The Classic Collection

U.S. STATE
QUILT·BLOCKS

By The Staff of WORKBASKET Magazine

Kansas City, Missouri

Second Printing
Third Printing

ATTENTION: SCHOOLS AND BUSINESS FIRMS
KC Publishing books are available at quantity discounts for bulk purchases for educational, business or sales promotional use. Call Judy Dawson at (816) 531-5730.

Printed in the United States of America

LIBRARY OF CONGRESS CATALOGING IN PUBLICATION DATA

U.S. state quilt blocks/by the staff of Workbasket magazine.
1. Quilting – United States.   I. Workbasket.   II. Title.   III. Title: U.S. state quilt blocks.
TT835.E465 1988   746.46'0973 – dc19   87-34844
ISBN 0-86675-300-1   CIP

TABLE OF CONTENTS

INTRODUCTION

In 1936, The WORKBASKET first published a delightful collection of state quilt patterns for use as coverlets, pillows, comforters, bedspreads, wall hangings and any of the many uses the imaginative quilter can conceive. The collection proved very popular with these early readers. Almost unbelievably, requests for reprints of the patterns were received for decades after their original publication.

Because of the lasting interest in the state quilt collection, The WORKBASKET staff revised the original patterns, updating the collection to include Alaska and Hawaii. To celebrate the 50th anniversary of The WORKBASKET, the series was reprinted over a two and a half year period.

Once again, the patterns met with the resounding approval of The WORKBASKET readers. Requests for reprints of missed patterns or the entire collection have been received on a daily basis since the series was completed in May, 1987. In response to this overwhelming demand, all 50 patterns have been collected for the first time in this single volume.

In addition to the patterns, we have included a special section from *Aunt Ellen's Quilting Handbook* on basic quilting instructions and techniques. This chapter will enable even the novice quilter to create any of the 50 projects in this book. While the section is intended primarily for the beginner quilter, it is our hope that more experienced quilters will also find something of value to increase their skill and enjoyment of the craft.

BASIC QUILTING INSTRUCTIONS

UNDERSTANDING THE TERMINOLOGY

A basic quilt by simple definition consists of three distinct layers; the "top" is sewn securely to the "backing" with the "filler" sandwiched between.

There are three main types of quilts, *Pieced, Appliquéd* and *Plain.* From these, many variations have evolved over the centuries. The names apply to the construction and ornamentation of the "tops."

Pieced Quilts are made by sewing pieces of material together to form the tops. Pieced quilts are primarily American in origin. In pioneer days, material of any kind was hard to get. Fabric scraps, remnants and worn out clothing were saved out of necessity for patching and quilt making. If these pieces were sewn together randomly as they fit, they formed a *Crazy Quilt,* whose principal virtue was warmth, with beauty a secondary consideration. When pieces were selected carefully by color, then cut to exact shapes and sizes to form a specific design, they were known as *Patchwork Quilts.* Simple squares, triangles, diamonds, circles and polygons were used to form typical patchwork designs.

Appliquéd Quilts, sometimes called *Laid On Quilts,* feature tops made by cutting shapes from one fabric and sewing them into place on another piece of fabric forming a design or decoration. Also called "Patch On Patch," they require more fabric than a pieced quilt.

Appliqués are occasionally sewn to pieced or plain quilts as added ornamentation. Flowers, animals, birds, stars and scrolls are examples of typical appliqué designs. Stuffed appliqué is a form of trapunto in which parts of the overall design are stuffed with filler or cordage in order to raise them above the surface of the quilt top.

Plain Quilts employ simple, one-piece tops upon which designs may be quilted or elaborately embroidered with intricate stitching. Trapunto is widely used in the lavish embellishment of Plain Quilts, which are considered the crown jewels of the quilt making art. Elegant simplicity is achieved by quilting designs on an all white quilt using white thread.

Here alphabetically are quilt making terms and their meanings.

APPLIQUÉ
A piece of fabric sewn to a larger one by embroidery or hemstitching.
BACKING
The bottom layer of a quilt, usually muslin or a solid pastel colored sheet.
BASTING
Sewing fabric with long loose stitches in order to hold in place temporarily.
BINDING
A narrow strip of fabric used to cover and hold the open edges of a quilt to prevent raveling.

BLOCK
A geometric unit of a quilt top design usually composed of individual pieces of fabric sewn together in a pattern.
BORDER
A broad strip of material along all sides of a finished quilt.
COMFORTER
An especially thick quilt, often reversible, and usually a solid color.
COVERLET
Generally a quilt large enough to cover a bed and pillows used with a dust ruffle to reach the floor.
FILLER
Cotton batting, polyester, goose down or other fluffy material sandwiched between the top and the backing of a quilt to provide warm insulation and add height to the top.
FOUNDATION BLOCK
A solid piece of fabric to which individual pieces of fabric are sewn in a pattern to form a block in the overall design of the top.
LATTICEWORK
Lengths of fabric added to separate or frame pattern blocks. Some quilters call it "sashing" or "stripping."
MITER
A seam cut at an angle; for example, joining two pieces to form a corner.
PATCH
Can mean either a small piece of fabric or a block.
PATCHWORK
Designs formed by small pieces sewn together.

QUILT STITCH
Any sewing stitch that penetrates all three layers of a quilt (top, filler and backing) and holds them together securely. It can range from a single tied stitch to a pattern of some fancy stitch.
SETTING
Stitching together all the blocks of a quilt top in the overall pattern. Or, laying out the blocks in desired order, adding latticework (sashing), and stitching together the entire top.
SELVAGE
The bound edge on both sides of a bolt of fabric that is finished off to prevent raveling.
TEMPLATE
A pattern, often cut from cardboard or plastic, for tracing a design onto fabric.
TIED QUILT
One in which the top, filler and backing are fastened together with single stitches securely knotted. Especially thick quilts and comforters are tied this way.
TOP
The upper layer or facing of a quilt consisting of a single piece of fabric, multiple pieces, appliqués, embroidered fabric or any combination of these.

These are some of the more common terms used in quilting and as you read further you will find still more. In some parts of the country different terms are used to describe the same thing. Latticework vs. sashing is one example. It is impossible to list all combinations and colloquialisms in this limited space.

CHOOSING EQUIPMENT

In order to make a quilt one certainly needs pins, needles and scissors. However, your enjoyment of quilting will be heightened if you have tools and accessories especially made for quilting. This chapter briefly discusses the various types of equipment available so you can be aware of the many options and plan accordingly.
Quilting Frames
Full size quilting frames hold the work even and flat as well as allowing more

than one person to quilt at the same time. Full size frames can be made or purchased, and usually are adjustable in both length and width for making various size quilts. To bring the frame to a comfortable sewing height, frames can be rested on the backs of chairs, mounted on carpenter's horses, or even suspended from the ceiling. **Lap Frames** and **Quilting Hoops** are convenient for apartment quilting and sew-as-you-go methods. They are especially useful for working small areas, but the quilter must beware of bunching and unevenness, particularly when working with a hoop.

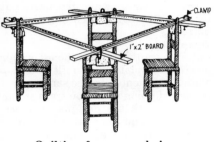

Quilting frame on chairs

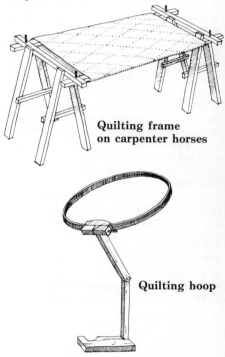

Quilting frame on carpenter horses

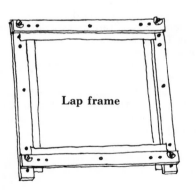

Lap frame

Quilting hoop

Sewing Machine

As long as the machine used is clean, dependable and in good working condition, it need not have zigzag or other fancy stitch capabilities unless machine embroidery is required. Ask your sewing machine dealer to see quilting accessories, such as a quilting foot, that will fit your machine.

Ironing Board

An ironing board is a necessity for pressing seams, steaming out wrinkles and creases and smoothing patchwork. A board with adjustable height can also be used as an extension table to hold the bulk of a quilt, if you are quilting with a sewing machine.

Needles

For hand sewing quilts, the most popular sizes are 7, 8 and 9 "betweens," which are shorter and stronger than the sharps used for embroidery and appliqué work. For machine quilting, the preference is size 14 or size 80 for most quilt work, with a size 16 or size 90 for thick quilts.

Thimble
Metal, leather or plastic are all popular. Rubber thumb and finger stalls can also serve as thimbles and have the added advantage of being a great help in pulling a needle through the multiple thicknesses in quilting.

Beeswax
Treating thread with beeswax or paraffin makes it stronger and easier to pull through the layers of a quilt.

Pins
Glass-headed pins and T-pins generally are preferred over common straight pins because they are easier to see and, being longer, hold more material. Safety pins of various sizes are particularly helpful in hoop quilting.

Scissors
Have available sharp shears for cutting patterns and batting, along with a small pair for snipping threads and other minor cuts.

Markers
Pencils, water-soluble markers and tailor's chalk are excellent for drawing quilting designs on fabric because such markings can then be washed away with ease.

Measures
Laying out materials for cutting and figuring yardage requires a ruler, yardstick, meterstick or tape measure.

Compass
Indispensable in drawing circular patterns or "walking off" equal distances.

Protractor
Necessary for drawing geometric patterns with angles such as diamond patterns.

Templates
Cut from cardboard, pasteboard or light plastic, templates of quilt patterns might be cemented to fine sandpaper to prevent slipping while you trace around them to mark the designs on fabric. Always cut a quilting pattern template ¼ inch large on all sides for seam allowances.

Cutting Board
A large, smooth board ruled in 1 inch squares to facilitate measuring and cutting fabric squarely.

Miscellany
Other useful items include graph paper for creating one's own designs; crayons for coloring designs; paper for making patterns, a tracing wheel and dressmaker's carbon for copying patterns onto fabric.

SELECTING MATERIALS

Quilt making should be enjoyed at a relaxed and easy pace. To ensure this, take time to select fabrics and fillers that are easy to cut and sew together. Here are a few suggestions to help you in choosing materials that not only are easier to work with, but also will make a quilt that is longer lasting and more serviceable.

QUILT FABRIC PREFERENCES

A quilt is a "showpiece" to be seen and admired, so extra care should be taken in selecting material for it. Colorfast, preshrunk, soft, smooth, wrinkle-resistant materials that will not ravel are a must. Fabrics of 100 percent cotton are highly recommended, with cotton blends second in popularity. If you buy material that is stiff with sizing, washing it well before using will make your needlework easier. It is best to purchase too much, rather than just enough material, to allow for layout or cutting errors. Also fabric colors vary from bolt to bolt and you may never be able to get a perfect match.

Certain materials are more suitable for being cut into patches and appliqué designs for the quilt top. Among these are calico, gingham, broadcloth and percale. Muslin, broadcloth, percale, cambric, flannel or challis are good choices for large areas and quilt backings.

If you intend to construct your quilt from "rag bag scraps," it is best not to mix different fabrics such as cottons with silks or rayons. Shrinkage at different rates will cause puckering. Some synthetics also ravel easily. Tightly woven fabrics should be avoided because they make needlework difficult and put undue strain on the thread and surrounding patches of lighter weight fabric.

Taking care in selecting good materials will be rewarded in the long run with a more serviceable quilt that will look better longer.

POPULAR QUILT FILLERS

Modern day quilt fillers or batting are far superior to the rags and corn shucks used in many early American quilts. Manmade synthetic fibers lead the way and are available in sheets of various sizes and thicknesses. The fibers in these snow-white polyester batts are locked together to prevent bunching and wadding while remaining light, puffy and springy. An imperceptible glazing holds surface fibers and prevents them from working through the quilt top or the

backing. Synthetics launder beautifully and dry fast. Cotton batting also is available in various sizes and thicknesses. It must be quilted closely because of its tendency to wad and shift. Cotton is easier to use than synthetics where thinning down, bevelling or stuffing appliqués are involved. Combed wool is preferred where warmth is most important. Wool is springier than cotton, but will shrink and has a natural oil content. Therefore, prewashing in hot water to preshrink the fibers and remove excess oil is important, unless the quilt will be dry cleaned or washed in cold water.

QUILTING THREAD

It's wise to choose high quality thread that is especially made for quilting. There are primarily two choices, each available in white and a variety of colors. Cotton quilting thread is one choice and, like the stronger cotton covered polyester core thread, is usually readily available in different strengths or weights, the most popular being between 50 and 70. Some experienced quilters soak their quilting thread in melted paraffin before use to make it pull through the multiple layers of a quilt easier and to eliminate knotting. If you are using a sewing machine use regular machine sewing thread rather than quilting thread. Choose cotton thread for cotton fabrics and cotton wrapped polyester for cotton blends and synthetics.

ESTIMATING MATERIAL NEEDS

There are many ways to calculate how much fabric and filler you will need to complete a particular quilt. If you are an experienced quilter you probably have your own method. Beginners may find the following suggestions helpful.

Most quilts are made to fit a particular bed or size of bed. While mattress sizes may vary slightly from brand to brand, the following chart provides you with a close approximation of standard mattress sizes in both inches and centimeters.

Mattress Size	Width	Length
Bassinet	13 in.	28 in.
	32.5 cm.	70 cm.
Crib	27 in.	54 in.
	67.5 cm.	135 cm.
Youth	33 in.	66 in.
	82.5 cm.	165 cm.
Twin or Bunk	39 in.	75 in.
	97.5 cm.	187.5 cm.
Single	36 in.	75 in.
	90 cm.	187.5 cm.
Long Twin	39 in.	80 in.
	97.5 cm.	200 cm.
Three Quarter	48 in.	72 in.
	120 cm.	180 cm.
Double	54 in.	75 in.
	135 cm.	187.5 cm.
Queen	60 in.	80 in.
	150 cm.	200 cm.
King	76 in.	80 in.
	190 cm.	200 cm.

Because mattresses may vary slightly in size, it is best to measure the bed yourself. If you measure in inches, multiply by 2.5 to convert to centimeters. Divide centimeters by 2.5 to convert to inches.

The first step in calculating yardage is to determine the overall quilt size. In addition to area of the top of the mattress, decide whether the quilt is also to cover bed pillows, if it is to drape to the floor on each side and how much the quilt is to drape over the foot end of the bed. These measurements should be added to the mattress top measurements and will give you a good idea of how much backing you will need. Using these dimensions, draw the overall outline of your quilt to scale on graph paper,

marking in the actual dimensions for reference. Inside this overall outline lightly draw the mattress top area as a further reference.

Computing the amount of fabric needed for the quilt top is the next step. For making a plain or embroidered quilt, this process is simple, for you need the same amount as for the backing. For a crazy quilt, provide enough pieces of top fabric to completely cover the backing plus enough extra for seam allowance. A good way to check quantity before beginning, if you are using remnants, is to lay out pieces on a bedsheet with plenty of overlap for seam allowance and cutting waste. If purchasing fabric for the top of a crazy quilt, decide how many colors or fabrics you will use in total; determine what percent or fraction of the top each will be allotted in total yardage, seams and all, and purchase accordingly.

To estimate the fabric needs for the top of a patchwork or pieced quilt with a definite design, first determine the exact size and number of design blocks needed for the overall design. Then measure out the area left for borders, latticework or sashing. These now can be drawn in proper scale on a graph paper chart. Figuring the yardage for solid areas of border and latticework (sashing) with allowance for seams is simple arithmetic. Figuring the yardage for the individual pieces of the design blocks can be simplified by actually cutting the design pieces out of scrap paper in full size, including allowance for seams. Now mark all the pieces that will be in the same color with crayon perhaps, and lay them out on a piece of paper exactly 36 inches square (one yard). Place the pieces as close together as you can, just as you would if you intended to cut out a pattern, to see how many pieces you can get from one yard of fabric. Then determine how much yardage is required of that particular fabric and color to provide for all the pieces in the overall design. Even cottons labeled preshrunk might shrink two to three percent, so it is well to allow a little extra fabric for shrinkage and for miscuts. Two inches per yard is a realistic allowance.

Once the top and backing yardage is computed and charted for reference, determine whether the filling will be used throughout the quilt or only in the portion covering the mattress. Enter this information on your chart and add it to your shopping list.

MAKING AND USING PATTERNS

In quilt making, patterns are used for two very different operations. There are patterns for appliqué designs or for patchwork to make up the quilt top. There are also patterns for the actual quilting process, which is stitching the quilt top to the quilt backing with the filler sandwiched between. The exception is Crazy Quilt, where the top has no pre-planned pattern, and quilting is usually done along seam lines of the random pieces of the top.

Patterns are available from a variety of sources besides The WORKBASKET Magazine such as books, quilt shops and mail order firms. You can trace patterns of existing quilts or perhaps create your own original designs. Tissue or tracing paper is recommended for tracings to leave the original intact for future reference. Allowing ¼ inch all around each individual piece for seam allowance, tracings can be transferred directly to the fabric with dressmaker's carbon. However, it is preferable to make templates by transferring the pattern to heavy cardboard, artboard or thin plastics. Cementing fine sandpaper to the backs of templates makes them skid-proof. Mark on top of each template the name of the pattern, the color and the number of pieces required of that particular shape to save time and avoid cutting errors.

For creating your own designs or drafting patterns larger or smaller than the original pattern, graph paper is indispensable. Here is a practical way to enlarge a pattern from a reduced size shown in a book to the full size needed for cutting.

First trace the original onto graph paper with ¼ inch squares. Number the squares on the left side from the bottom from 1 up. Then letter the squares from left to right across the top: A, B, C, etc. To make the example simple, let's say the design is now 8 inches long and 5 inches wide and the actual full size you want is to be double that or 16 by 10. The next step is to take a large sheet of paper and rule it into perfect ½ inch squares numbered and lettered to match the smaller size drawing. A T-square is a great help in making your squares true and your lines straight. Now square by square, A1, A2 and so on, draw on your double size graph the same pattern lines that appear on the original grid. Practice this technique on just a few squares until you've mastered it. Note that *you* control the size of the squares in the final graph, so it's a matter of determining how much larger or smaller than the original you want the pattern to be.

Drawing the straight lines of triangles, diamonds and rectangles is easy, but drawing accurate curves and circles can be difficult. Dishes and glassware can be useful tools in making these curves accurately. Once the final pattern drawing is completed, a template can be made from it.

FOLDING AND CUTTING TECHNIQUES

One of the most important steps in quilt making is cutting materials accurately so the parts fit together smoothly. A large, flat area such as a cutting board, or a dining room table with extension leaves in place, or even the floor, make suitable cutting surfaces. A sharp pair of scissors with blades at least four inches long is another requirement. The cardinal rule is *cut,* don't tear.

When using remnants or wrinkled goods, be sure to iron the fabric because even slight wrinkling can cause cutting errors. The first step in working with new material is to cut off the selvage. Fabric can be folded and securely pinned to cut two identical pieces. Cutting with more than two layers can cause distortions. Consider the grain of the material in relation to the design as there are strength advantages to having the grain run with the long dimension of your design pieces. Care should be taken to place your tracing templates so you get the proper graining, and if you are using a patterned fabric, the right direction of the print.

The actual cutting should be done with sharp scissors or fabric shears to avoid fraying. Scissors should be held straight up and down when cutting through multiple layers so no bevelling occurs which would cause different layers to be distorted in shape or size. Once the cutting is completed, press the seam allowances on all pieces. At this point, it's a good idea to tally and bundle like pieces together to be sure of counts and to keep them from going astray. A tally slip for each group with count and placement information may prove very helpful during assembly.

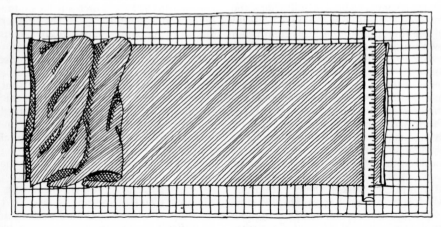

Lining up folded fabric on a cutting board

STITCHING TECHNIQUES

Only a few simple stitches are needed in quilt making and often the stitch used for a particular application is a matter of personal preference. Beginners will find it advantageous to practice these stitches on scrap material. Those who will be makng their quilts in part or entirely with their sewing machines will find this section helpful in considering machine settings to accomplish the same results as hand stitching wherever possible.

Back Stitch
Resembles machine stitching and is used to strengthen a seam. Make one running stitch, then take a stitch back to the beginning of the first stitch, thus overlapping each running stitch.

Buttonhole Stitch
An alternative to the hemming stitch in attaching appliqués, binding the edges of quilts, and the like. Insert needle through the work (as shown) and pull snug.

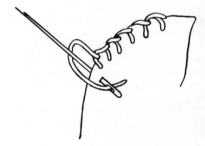

Basting
To temporarily hold fabric in place until final stitching can be done one can either use pins or stitches. For pin basting, it is well to place the pins with heads all facing away from you in one direction for ease in removing them as you put in permanent stitches by hand or by machine. Hand basting is accomplished by making long running stitches. On a machine not only lengthen your stitch but also loosen the tension as well.

Backlock Stitch
To fasten the last stitch in a row of stitches without tying knots, repeat the last stitch over itself several times.

Hemming Stitch
Used primarily to attach appliqués to quilt top blocks or wherever an almost hidden stitch is desirable in joining two pieces of fabric. Begin by bringing the needle up from the underside as close to the fold as possible, in order to hide the locking knot on the end of the thread. Now insert the needle in the background fabric as close to the first stitch as possible to keep the visible part of the stitch small. Slightly angle the needle to the side so when it emerges from the appliqué the spacing for the next stitch is hidden. For maximum strength, keep your hemming stitches close together and evenly spaced.

free hand. Working back and forth in this manner you may get two or three stitches on your needle before pulling it through. If you're working on a thicker quilt, again working toward you, insert the needle straight down through all three layers while holding the backing and lining up against the top with your free hand. When the needle comes through the backing, pull it completely through and reinsert it straight upward through the three layers about ⅛ inch nearer to you with your free hand and pull it clear with your working hand when it comes through the top. Tighten the stitch and continue. Quilting also can be done well on a sewing machine using a sharp needle and with thread tensions properly set.

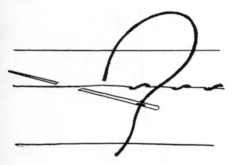

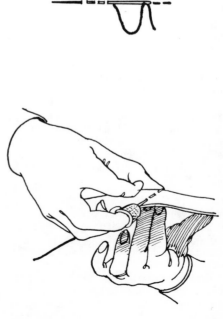

Quilting Stitch
While it might also be decorative, the primary function of the quilting stitch is to securely fasten the quilt top to the quilt backing and lock the quilt lining or filler in place. Six to ten short running stitches to the inch usually are used for quilting. If the quilt is relatively thin, working toward you, insert the needle through all three layers at a slight angle with your working hand while holding the backing and filler up against the top from underneath with your free hand. When you feel the needle come through the backing, guide it back up with the

Running Stitch

The running stitch is one of the most popular basic stitches used in quilt making. It is used in joining design pieces together into patches or blocks, in sewing blocks together, in attaching borders and in quilting. Using a single in-and-out motion, take several small, evenly spaced stitches on the needle before pulling the needle through and gently tightening the thread.

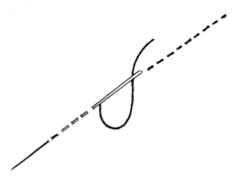

Tie Stitch

Extremely thick quilts or comforters may require a hand-tied stitch to fasten the quilt top, filler and backing together securely. A heavy, waxed thread, perhaps candle wicking, is used. With a large-eyed yarn needle, insert the thread down through all three layers; leave about ¼ inch of space and bring the thread back up through all three layers. Allowing about two inches of thread on each side, cut the thread, pull it snug and tie a square knot tightly. Ends now may be clipped to about one inch in length.

A variety of fancy stitches may also be used to quilt or to embroider the top of a quilt to make it prettier.

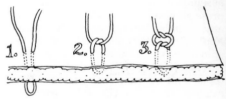

ASSEMBLING YOUR QUILT

There are various ways in which a quilt can be assembled. The traditional method involves three steps: sewing together, appliquéing or embroidering the top; stitching together the backing, if it is made of more than one piece; and quilting together the top, filler and backing on a full-size quilting frame. Many quilters prefer this method over all others.

Another method that has become popular in recent years is apartment or sew-as-you-go quilting. The advantage is that it can be done in a very small area and one can even carry the quilting along to work on in a waiting room or on a trip, for example. This method consists of sewing together, appliquéing or embroidering the top and cutting out a matching block of filler and one of the backing. Then, using a large quilting or embroidery hoop, or a lap frame, the actual quilting is done. When all the squares to make up the full-size quilt are completed, they are sewn together. Yet another method is to assemble the top, filler and backing in block-wide strips which are then sewn together to form the finished quilt. These last two methods lend themselves well to using a sewing machine for part or all of the steps. From these basic methods of quilting American ingenuity has fostered many variations. Regardless of the method you choose, here are helpful suggestions.

Sew-as-you-go block

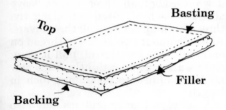

One of the judging points of a fine quilt is that it is neatly and smoothly assembled. Keep your iron handy to press all seams to one side and iron out any wrinkles before joining the blocks. Your finished quilt will be much smoother as a result.

When joining individual pieces of the top of a pieced quilt, first pin the corners exactly, then pin the sides together. Check both sides of the work for accuracy before sewing. After sewing together with short running stitches, press the seams flat to prevent wrinkling or curling which could show through the top after it has been quilted. Basting is especially important in appliqué to be sure that all the seam allowances are flat and smooth before you begin to appliqué the design pieces in place.

Before setting a quilt (sewing the top together), it's a good idea to lay the blocks, strips or pieces out on the bed on which it will be used both to try the fit and to check the visual effect. Allow for seaming by overlapping if necessary. This gives you the opportunity to adjust the dimensions of latticework, borders or flounces before they are added in order to get the best possible fit. Once you are satisfied with how the top lays,

baste the quilt together a portion at a time by joining corners first, then seams. Carefully stitch the top together with short running stitches along the seams by hand or machine. Trim off any excess material, then press the top to make quilting easier.

Should your quilt's design call for Trapunto (Italian quilting), English padding or stuffed appliqué, these decorations should be added before the top is laid on the filler and backing. These unique forms of quilting are especially popular in the South where quilt warmth is not important and where filler may not be added. In each case these involve two pieces of fabric stitched together with filler, cording or yarn stuffed or threaded in between to raise the design above the surrounding surface of the top as an added design. Shown below are typical examples:

Trapunto

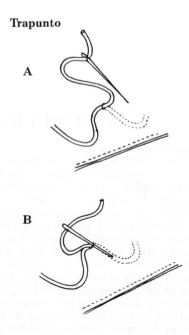

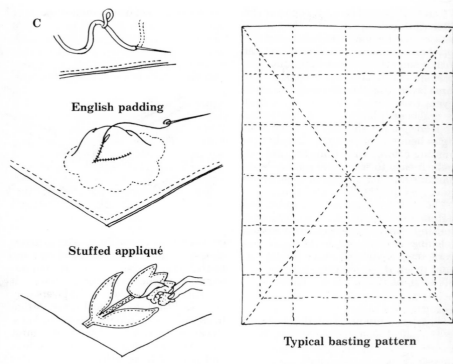

English padding

Stuffed appliqué

Typical basting pattern

The design that the actual quilt stitching is to follow usually is marked on the top before it is put into a quilting frame or hoop. No marking is needed if quilting will be done along the seam lines of the design of a patchwork quilt, or around the outlines of a major appliqué. Marking is very important on plain quilts, in large open spaces, or on wide latticework, where no guidelines already exist. Decorative quilting patterns should be close enough together to hold the filler securely in place. However, quilting that is too close together mats down the filler, which cuts down its insulating qualities and decreases warmth.

As a general rule, straight line quilting designs are used in open areas or plain blocks to set off curving designs in pieced or appliquéd quilts. Swirls and curved quilting designs are chosen to effectively contrast with straight line appliqués or piecework designs.

Preparing the fabric for quilting is extremely important. Place the backing wrong side up on a large, clean, flat surface. The grain of the backing should run the same direction as the grain in the top. This helps to minimize the possibility of puckering. Take pains to see that all corners are square and all sides are straight.

Place the filler on top of the backing. In joining sections of filler, cut away the upper half from one edge and the lower half from the other. Overlap the two half thicknesses and baste together with long even stitches. Care should be taken not to distort the squareness of the backing when laying the filler on it.

Carefully place the quilt top over the filler, right side up. Recheck the squareness of the backing, the filler and the top. Accuracy here will be rewarded later with a smooth, symmetrical quilt. The final step in this process is to baste the three layers together. Pinning the three layers together at the corners and at several other places prevents the layers from creeping or shifting while the basting is being done. Using a sharply contrasting colored thread for basting will make it easy to see and to remove later. Basting stitches and pins may be removed as quilting is completed.

The quilt body can now be rolled and fastened to a quilt frame, worked on a quilting hoop, or stitched on a sewing machine. Sewing will be easier if you work toward yourself from the center, right to left if you are right-handed, and left to right if you are left-handed.

Example of frame mounting

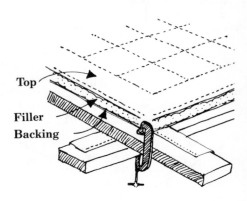

on your sewing machine. The stitches should be about one-sixteenth inch long, so that the top doesn't creep. Keep quilting stitches short and evenly spaced. If the stitches are too loose, the layers may shift. Quilting should be done on design lines and on or parallel to seam lines. Because the front and back of a quilt should be smooth and knot free, the first and last quilting stitches in a series should be firmly secured with lock stitches. Quilting should not be done within two inches of the outside edges to allow addition of a smooth, pucker-free binding.

Particularly thick quilts or comforters are extremely difficult if not impossible to quilt. These are better tied every three to six inches in all directions.

The final step in quilt construction is binding the edges. One way is to slightly trim the backing, extend the top over it, roll ¼ inch of the top under to form a hemline and closely hemstitch the top to the backing. Another way is to reverse the process and lap the backing over the top. A third way is to whipstitch the top and backing together with a loose buttonhole stitch, adding a long strip of border hemmed to both top and backing.

Rolling a quilt

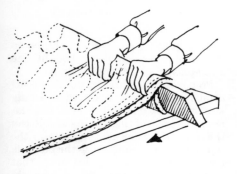

If you are a beginner, baste together a small block of topping fabric, filler and backing to practice the quilting stitch you intend to use. You may find the up-and-down quilting stitch works better for you than the in-and-out running stitch, for example. A practice block is a great help in proper stitch regulation

CARE OF QUILTS

After all the time and work involved in making a quilt, the utmost care should be taken to preserve its beauty. Many people feel you age quilts five years each time you wash them, but from time to time it is necessary to do so. Thorough vacuuming with the brush attachment is helpful, along with frequent airings. Be sure to hang the quilt over several clotheslines.

Before you wash your quilt, be sure fabrics are colorfast and preshrunk. This should have been done before the quilt was made. Also check for any tears or worn spots and mend these before washing.

If your quilt has cotton batting, it should be quilted with close stitches to hold the quilt and the filler together.

Since a washing machine agitates and pulls the quilt too much, hand washing is recommended. Using mild, sudsy water in a large sink or tub, gently agitate the quilt with your hands. After washing, several rinses will be necessary to remove all soap. Continue refilling and emptying the tub until rinse water is clear. Do not wring, but gently squeeze as much water out as possible. Don't pick up a wet quilt. After pressing the water out, wrap the quilt in several beach towels to absorb the excess moisture. Hang the quilt on a drying rack or over several clotheslines so that it hangs horizontally across the top of the lines. **Do not** hang the quilt from one end. An alternative to hanging it is to place it on a sheet on the grass to dry. Cover it with another sheet to protect it.

SPECIAL INSTRUCTIONS

Quilting has been an enjoyable pastime for hundreds of years. Using the state quilt patterns, create a quilt uniquely your own to treasure and enjoy for years to come.

Aunt Ellen said over 50 years ago, "A really pretty quilt will result if you repeat only one block, perhaps that of your own state." If you decide to do that, you may want to alternate plain and patchwork blocks, make an all-over design, or use lattice strips between the blocks. Most of the patterns will give suggestions on the best usage of that particular design.

Each block is 12 inches square making it easy to mix or match blocks. A sampler quilt can be made using several state patterns. Choose the states you have lived in, perhaps those of your ancestors, maybe several states in your section of the country, or just choose the patterns you like. Identical lattice strips around each block will visually tie different patterns together. Using the same fabrics in each block will also help to unify the quilt.

Before beginning, read the entire pattern. Decide how many blocks you will need for your project. If you use lattice strips, remember to add the width of the strips when determining the number of blocks and the amount of fabric you will need.

Pattern pieces are given full size whenever possible. Add ¼ inch seam allowance on all sides of each piece, with the exception of the Hawaiian pattern piece.

The patterns are arranged by month as they were published in the series, with similar patterns in the same month. Happy quilting!

KENTUCKY · DELAWARE
ALABAMA

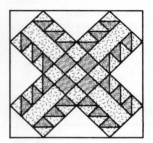

**KENTUCKY
CROSSROADS**

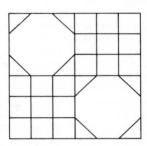

**DELAWARE
FLAGSTONES**

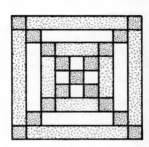

ALABAMA

KENTUCKY CROSSROADS

Made of 3 different fabrics, you will need 5 light 1⅓ inch squares, 4 dark 1⅓ inch squares, 24 dark and 24 light triangles (made from 1⅓ inch square pattern cut in half diagonally), 4 white triangles (½ of 3 inch square), 4 white triangles (½ of 6 inch square) and 4 light rectangular 1⅓ x 4 inch strips. **Add ¼ inch seam allowance on all sides of each pattern.**

Assemble 9-patch center first, by working 3 strips of 3 squares to form center square. Sew light triangles to dark triangles to form squares. Three squares equal 1 strip. Place 2 of each of the "triangle" strips with a solid strip to form a square. Sew square on each side of 9-patch. Fill in corners and edges with triangles, medium size ones in corners and larger ones on the side edges.

This pattern makes a good all-over design without any lattice strips.

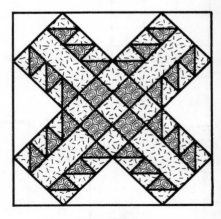

**KENTUCKY
CROSSROADS**

White   Dark   Print

DELAWARE FLAGSTONES

Only 2 fabrics are used for this block, based on 9-patch. You will need 10 white 2 inch squares, 8 dark 2 inch squares, 8 dark triangles (½ of 2 inch square) and 2 white 6 inch hexagons. **Add ¼ inch seam allowance on all sides of all patterns.**

Work two 9-patch squares, by working 3 strips of 3 squares and then joining to form a square. Piece triangles to corners of hexagons to form squares. Join squares to complete block.

ALABAMA

A 9-patch forms the center of this block. You will need 17 dark 1⅓ inch squares, 4 light 1⅓ inch squares, 4 medium 9⅓ x 1⅓ inch strips, 4 light 6⅔ x 1⅓ inch strips and 4 medium 4 x 1⅓ inch strips. **Add ¼ inch seam allowance on all sides of each pattern.**

Sew 3 strips of 3 alternating squares to form center 9-patch. Starting with shortest strips, add to center. Fill in corners with dark squares. Repeat with other strips and squares.

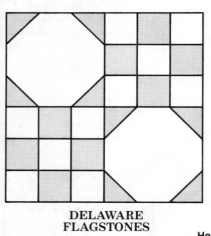

**DELAWARE
FLAGSTONES**

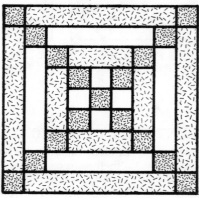

ALABAMA

| | White |
| | Dark |

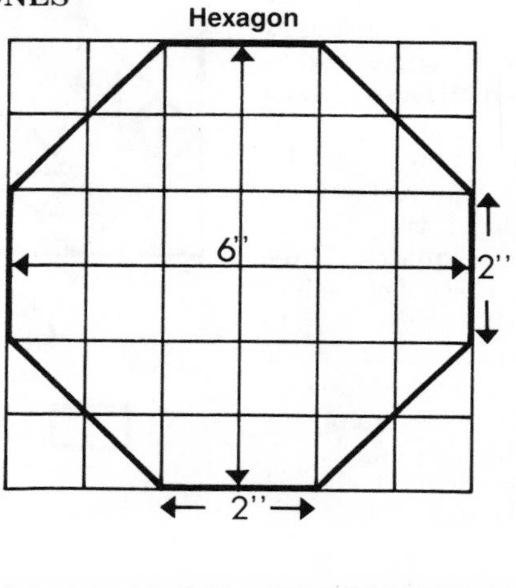

Hexagon

6"

2"

2"

	White
	Medium
	Dark

MISSOURI · NEW MEXICO SOUTH CAROLINA

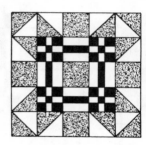

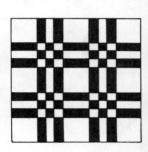

MISSOURI PUZZLE

NEW MEXICO STAR

SOUTH CAROLINA ALBUM

The state patterns of Missouri, New Mexico and South Carolina all feature 9-patch. The Missouri Puzzle and New Mexico Star are the same except for color reversal. Both feature triangles along with the squares. South Carolina's Album uses rectangular strips with the squares.

MISSOURI PUZZLE & NEW MEXICO STAR

Missouri and **New Mexico** use 3 fabrics. Pieces are given for the Missouri Puzzle with the color changes for New Mexico Star in parentheses. You will need 5 white (light) large squares, 20 white (dark) small squares, 16 dark (white) small squares, 8 dark (white) rectangles and 4 white (dark) rectangles. Both need 12 white and 12 light triangles.

Assemble 9-patch squares using smaller squares. Sew triangles to form squares; sew rectangles to form squares.

Sew squares to form strips as shown in diagram. Sew 5 strips together to complete block.

SOUTH CAROLINA ALBUM

South Carolina's block uses only 2 fabrics. You will need 9 white large squares, 20 white small squares, 16 dark small squares, 24 dark rectangles and 12 white rectangles. Sew rectangles to form squares, smaller squares to form 9-patch squares. Sew squares into 5 strips; sew strips together.

Note: Large square: 2.4 inches square; small square: .8 inch square; rectangles: 2.4 x .8 inches; triangles: ½ of 2.4 inch square. Decimal measurements are necessary to insure a 12 inch block. Use a ruler with tenths or cut 2.4 inches just under 2½ inches. Cut .8 inch just over ¾ inch. **Add ¼ inch seam allowance on all pieces.**

Add ¼ inch seam allowance on all pieces.

MISSOURI PUZZLE

5 white large squares
20 white small squares
16 dark small squares
8 dark rectangles
4 white rectangles
12 white triangles
12 light triangles

NEW MEXICO STAR

5 light large squares
20 dark small squares
16 white small squares
8 white rectangles
4 dark rectangles
12 white triangles
12 light triangles

☐ White

▨ Print

■ Dark

9 white large squares
20 white small squares
16 dark small squares
24 dark rectangles
12 white rectangles

SOUTH CAROLINA ALBUM

CONNECTICUT
LOUISIANA · VIRGINIA

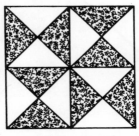

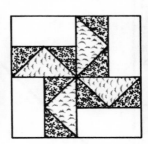

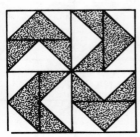

**CONNECTICUT
YANKEE PUZZLE**

LOUISIANA

**VIRGINIA
REEL**

Connecticut, Louisiana and Virginia's state quilt blocks all use the same pattern pieces. All pattern pieces are given full size; **add ¼ inch seam allowance on each side of all patterns.** The fabric color and number of pieces needed for each block are listed on each pattern piece.

CONNECTICUT
YANKEE PUZZLE

Connecticut's Yankee Puzzle uses 2 fabrics and only the large triangle. Sew each of the white triangles to a dark triangle to form a larger triangle. Then sew two of the larger triangles together to form a 6 inch square. Four squares complete the block. See the diagram for placement.

LOUISIANA

The **Louisiana** block uses 3 fabrics and is the only block to use the rectangle. Sew 2 smaller triangles to each larger triangle to form a rectangle. Join the white rectangle to this rectangle, forming a 6 inch block. Sew 4 blocks together as shown in diagram.

VIRGINIA REEL

Virginia Reel uses 2 colors. Sew 2 white triangles to each dark triangle; 2 dark triangles to each white triangle. Sew 2 strips together to form a 6 inch block; sew 4 blocks together as shown in diagram.

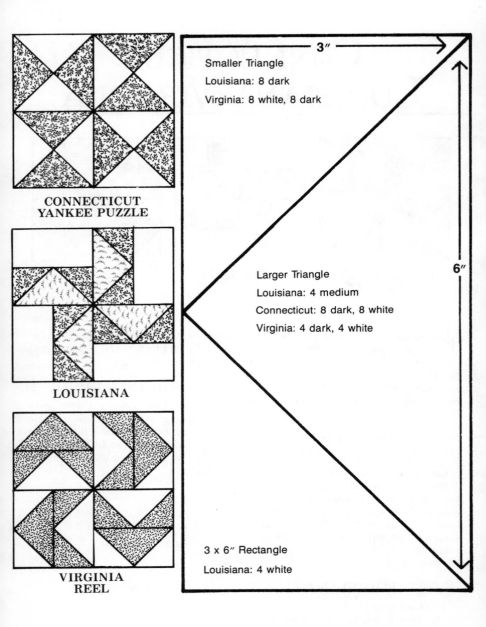

CONNECTICUT YANKEE PUZZLE

LOUISIANA

VIRGINIA REEL

Smaller Triangle
Louisiana: 8 dark
Virginia: 8 white, 8 dark

3″

6″

Larger Triangle
Louisiana: 4 medium
Connecticut: 8 dark, 8 white
Virginia: 4 dark, 4 white

3 x 6″ Rectangle
Louisiana: 4 white

ARKANSAS · CALIFORNIA
OREGON

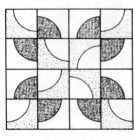

ARKANSAS TROUBLES

ROAD TO CALIFORNIA

OREGON TRAIL

The Arkansas, California and Oregon state quilts are all variations of the Drunkard's Path. The same two pieces (A and B) are used for all 3 quilts.

To join the A and B pieces to form a square, fold each piece in half and mark halfway on each curved seam line. Pin together at mark. Pin and sew one half; then, the other. Be sure sides line up evenly.

Each 12 inch block consists of 16 smaller squares arranged in four strips. On each pattern, check the diagram to determine the placement of A and B pieces.

ARKANSAS TROUBLES

Arkansas Troubles, an all-over pattern, uses white, print and dark fabric. Combine 8 dark A's with 8 white B's; 8 white A's with 8 print B's.

ROAD TO CALIFORNIA

Road to California, also an all-over pattern, is worked in white, medium and dark fabrics. Combine 8 white A's with 8 dark B's; 8 medium A's with 8 white B's.

OREGON TRAIL

The **Oregon Trail** is set with alternating plain blocks, with a dark B piece appliquéd in each corner. The effect is of a trail leading in every direction. It, too, uses a white, medium and dark fabric. Combine 8 white A's with 8 dark B's; 8 medium A's with 8 white B's.

**ROAD TO
CALIFORNIA**

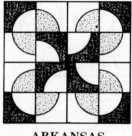

**ARKANSAS
TROUBLES**

**OREGON
TRAIL**

 White Dark Medium

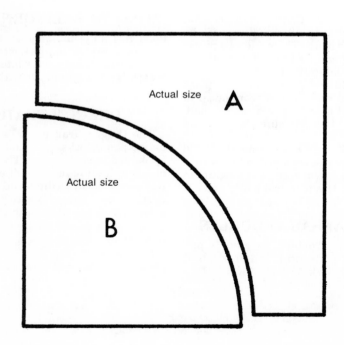

Actual size A

Actual size B

KANSAS
NORTH DAKOTA

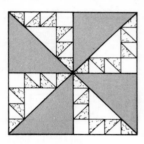

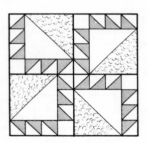

**KANSAS
TROUBLES**

**NORTH DAKOTA
BEAR PAW**

Kansas' and North Dakota's state blocks are both variations of Bear's Paw. All pattern pieces are given full size except the largest triangle in the Kansas pattern. Cut 4 dark triangles (½ of 6 inch square). **Be sure to add ¼ inch seam allowance on all pattern pieces.** The fabric color and number of pieces needed for each block are listed on the rest of the pattern pieces. Both Kansas and North Dakota use 3 fabrics: white, print and dark.

KANSAS TROUBLES

Kansas Troubles is made up in quarter squares. Begin with the small triangles, sewing print and white triangles together to form 4 small squares. Join these squares to the white square, forming a right angle; then, add a small print triangle at each end. Fit the medium-sized white triangle into the corner formed by the right angle. This will form a triangle equal in size to the large triangle. Join these 2 triangles together to

complete the quarter square. Sew 2 quarter squares together to form a half square. Two half squares will form the complete 12 inch square.

NORTH DAKOTA BEAR PAW

North Dakota's Bear Paw is also worked in quarter squares. Join a white and print triangle to form a square. Then sew each dark and white triangle together to form smaller squares. Sew 3 smaller squares together to form a rectangle. Sew rectangles to sides of white section of square. Fill in corner with small white square. Sew 2 quarter-squares together, as shown in diagram, to form half-square. Sew half squares together to form 12 inch square.

Both patterns can be set as all-over patterns or set with plain squares.

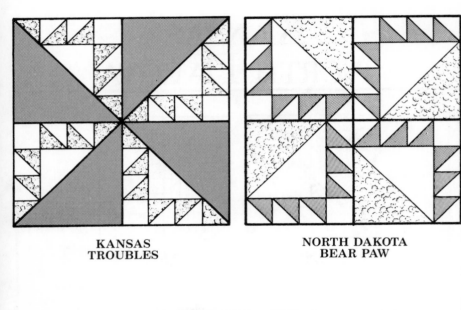

**KANSAS
TROUBLES**

**NORTH DAKOTA
BEAR PAW**

Dark   Print   White

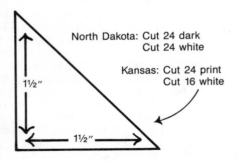

North Dakota: Cut 24 dark
Cut 24 white

Kansas: Cut 24 print
Cut 16 white

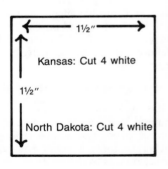

1½"

Kansas: Cut 4 white

1½"

North Dakota: Cut 4 white

Add ¼ inch seam allowance on all pieces.

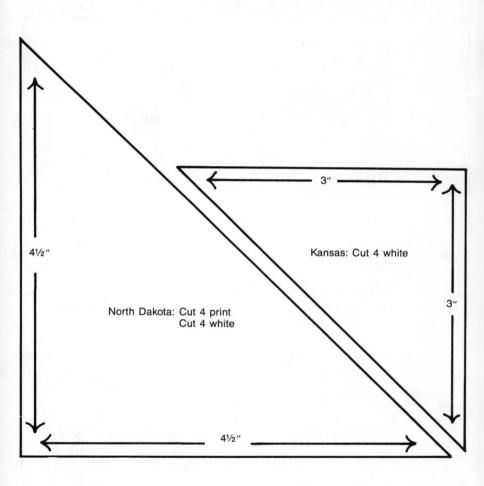

North Dakota: Cut 4 print
Cut 4 white

Kansas: Cut 4 white

MASSACHUSETTS · IOWA

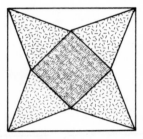

**MASSACHUSETTS
PRISCILLA**

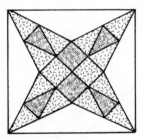

**IOWA
HAWKEYE STAR**

Massachusetts' and Iowa's state quilt blocks both have a center square and triangles to the corners of the completed 12 inch squares. Pattern pieces are given actual size; **add ¼ inch seam allowance on each side of all patterns.** Both states use 3 fabrics designated as dark, print and white.

MASSACHUSETTS PRISCILLA

Massachusetts' Priscilla is the easier of the two patterns. Cut one 5 inch dark square (not shown). Place Massachusetts' triangle on print fabric with xxx on fold and cut double. Cut 4 triangles and sew to each side of center square.

Then using same triangle pattern, place x on fold. Cutting double, cut 4 triangles from white fabric to fill in square. Massachusetts looks especially nice set with dark colored strips.

IOWA HAWKEYE STAR

Iowa's Hawkeye Star begins with a 3 inch center square made by joining two 1½ inch dark squares and two 1½ inch print squares. Each point is formed from 4 triangles (3 print and 1 dark) arranged as shown in diagram and then sewn to center square. Complete square by cutting the 4 fill-in triangles from white fabric doubled and pattern placed on fold. Sew in place.

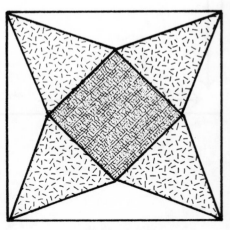

**MASSACHUSETTS
PRISCILLA**

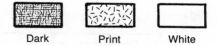

Dark   Print   White

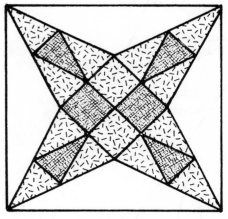

**IOWA
HAWKEYE STAR**

Cut 4

Actual size

5-inch square for Massachusetts not shown.

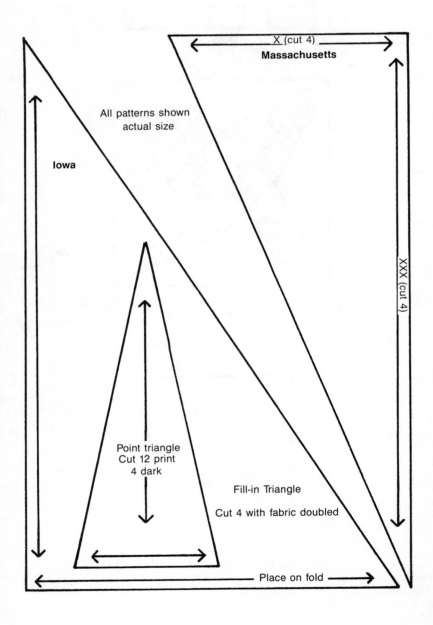

X (cut 4)

Massachusetts

All patterns shown
actual size

Iowa

XXX (cut 4)

Point triangle
Cut 12 print
4 dark

Fill-in Triangle

Cut 4 with fabric doubled

Place on fold →

INDIANA · GEORGIA

INDIANA
PUZZLE

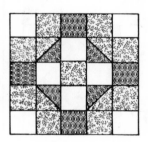

STATE OF
GEORGIA

Twenty-five smaller squares are used to create each of the Indiana and Georgia state quilt blocks. Both 12 inch blocks use only squares and triangles. Pattern pieces are given full size; **add ¼ inch seam allowance on all sides of each pattern.**

INDIANA PUZZLE

For the **Indiana Puzzle**, use only 2 fabrics, white and a print, and 3 pattern pieces, 2 squares and a triangle. Cut pieces as directed on the pattern pieces.

Sew the smaller squares to form 9 larger squares; sew triangles to form 12 larger squares. Following the diagram, assemble 5 squares to make a strip. The 5 strips will not all be the same so be careful when putting them together to form the completed block. The arrangement of the triangles will form a pinwheel pattern.

The Indiana Puzzle creates an interesting overall pattern or can be set with strips.

STATE OF GEORGIA

The **State of Georgia** block uses only 2 pattern pieces, the larger square and the triangle, and 3 fabrics. Sew each of the dark triangles to a medium triangle to form 4 squares. Following the diagram, assemble 5 squares to form a strip and then the strips to form the finished block. This block, too, looks good as an overall pattern or set with strips.

INDIANA PUZZLE

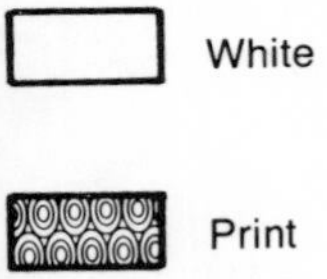

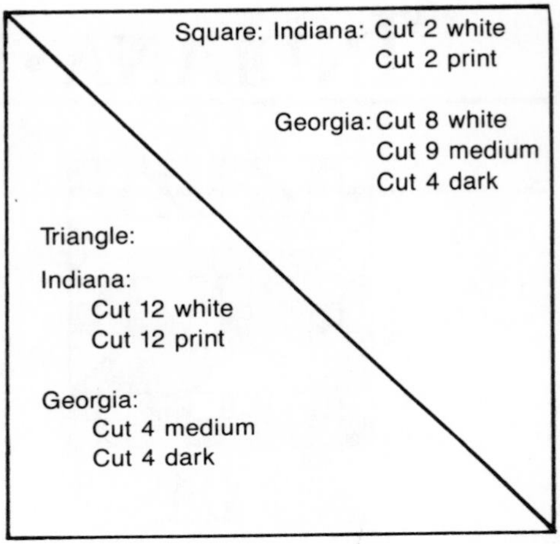

Square: Indiana: Cut 2 white
Cut 2 print

Georgia: Cut 8 white
Cut 9 medium
Cut 4 dark

Triangle:

Indiana:
Cut 12 white
Cut 12 print

Georgia:
Cut 4 medium
Cut 4 dark

White

Print

Add 1/4 inch seam
allowance on
all sides of
each pattern.

All pieces
actual size.

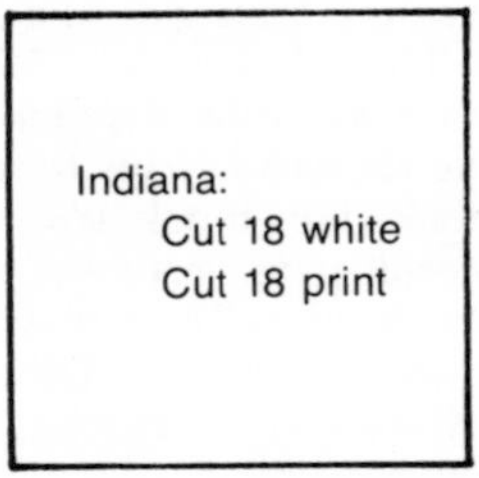

Indiana:
Cut 18 white
Cut 18 print

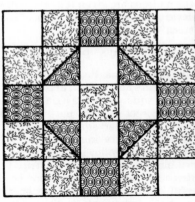

STATE OF GEORGIA

Medium   Dark   White

MARYLAND
WASHINGTON

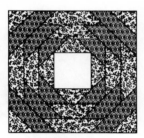

MARYLAND
WASHINGTON
PAVEMENT

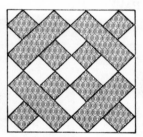

WASHINGTON
SIDEWALKS

Maryland's and Washington's state quilt patterns have similar names and both start from a center square. Washington's block, called Washington Sidewalks, is made of squares and rectangles whereas Maryland's block, called Washington Pavement, utilizes trapezoids. Both 12 inch blocks can be set with plain blocks or stripped with a border.

MARYLAND
WASHINGTON PAVEMENT

Washington Pavement, Maryland's block, is much like log cabin and pineapple blocks. You will need white, light print and dark print fabrics. The primary pieces are 6 trapezoid shaped pieces, each labeled A through F. Cut 4 of each size, cutting A, C and E from light print and B, D and F from dark print. From white, cut one 3½ inch square and 4 white triangles (½ of 2½ inch square). **Add ¼ inch seam allowance on all pieces.**

Begin with the 3½ inch square center.

Add trapezoid A to each of the 4 sides. Next add trapezoid B, followed by C, D, E and F. Finish with 4 white triangles in the corners.

WASHINGTON SIDEWALKS

Washington Sidewalks uses only 2 fabrics and is based on the actual size square pattern given. In addition to the squares, you will need 4 dark rectangles which can be formed by placing 3 squares together. The 12 triangles for the sides are ½ of a pattern square. The smaller triangle for the corners is given actual size. **Remember to add ¼ inch seam allowances.** The easiest way to form the center (which is a 9-patch) is to make 3 strips of 3 squares. See diagram for color placement. Sew all 3 strips together. Then add dark rectangles on each side. Sew the remaining squares in place, being careful to place the square in the middle of the rectangle. Add larger triangles to fill in sides; smaller triangles in the corners.

Actual size

MARYLAND
WASHINGTON
PAVEMENT

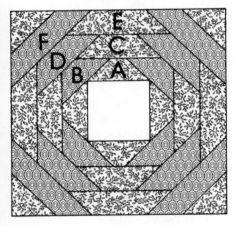

White   Light print   Dark print

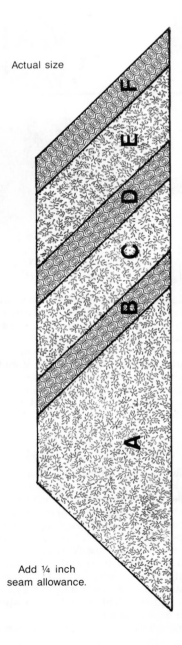

Add ¼ inch
seam allowance.

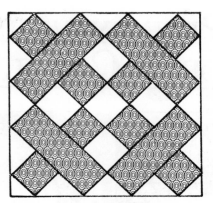

**WASHINGTON
SIDEWALKS**

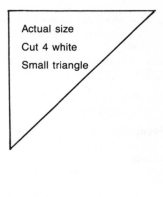

Actual size

Cut 8 dark

5 white

Actual size

Cut 4 white

Small triangle

Add ¼ inch
seam allowance.

PENNSYLVANIA
NORTH CAROLINA

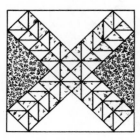

**PENNSYLVANIA
PINEAPPLE**

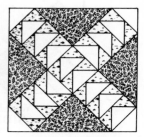

**NORTH CAROLINA
WILD GOOSE
CHASE**

Diagonal patterns are formed by triangles in both Pennsylvania's and North Carolina's state quilt blocks. Both 12 inch blocks are comprised of 3 different sized triangles.

PENNSYLVANIA
PINEAPPLE

Pennsylvania's Pineapple is usually worked with one or many prints, a dark fabric and white. You will need 36 small print triangles (½ of 1⅜ inch square), 36 small white triangles (½ of 1⅜ inch square), 4 medium white triangles (½ of 2 inch square), 2 large white triangles (½ of 5⅝ inch square) and 2 large dark triangles (½ of 5⅝ inch square). **Be sure to add ¼ inch seam allowance on all pattern pieces.**

Begin by sewing 36 squares of 1 print and 1 white triangle. Four squares form the center (Fig. 1). Join squares to form rectangles A, B, C and D (Fig. 2 and Fig. 3). Join completed rectangles to center as indicated; that is, join "A" rectangle

to "A" side of center, etc. Sew large triangles in place; complete corners with white medium triangles.

NORTH CAROLINA
WILD GOOSE CHASE

North Carolina's Wild Goose Chase is traditionally worked in 2 shades of blue and white. Pattern pieces are given actual size.

Sew 2 dark blue triangles to each of 14 white triangles forming rectangles. Eight rectangles with white "geese" flying in same direction form one diagonal. Three rectangles on each side complete second diagonal. Sew light blue triangles between diagonals. Add remaining 4 white triangles in corners.

Both blocks make interesting all-over designs.

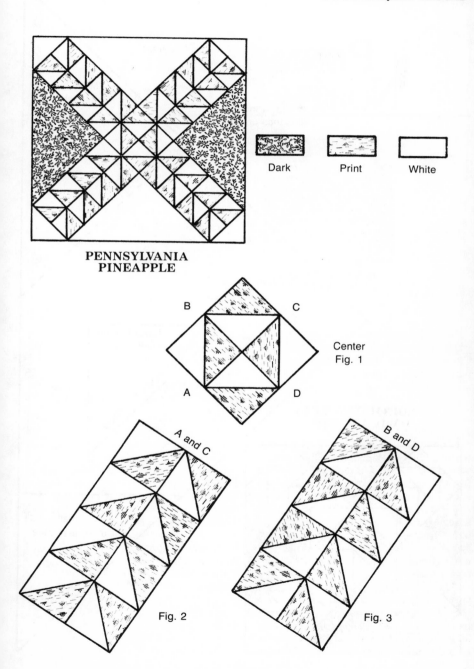

PENNSYLVANIA PINEAPPLE

Dark

Print

White

B   C

Center
Fig. 1

A   D

A and C

B and D

Fig. 2

Fig. 3

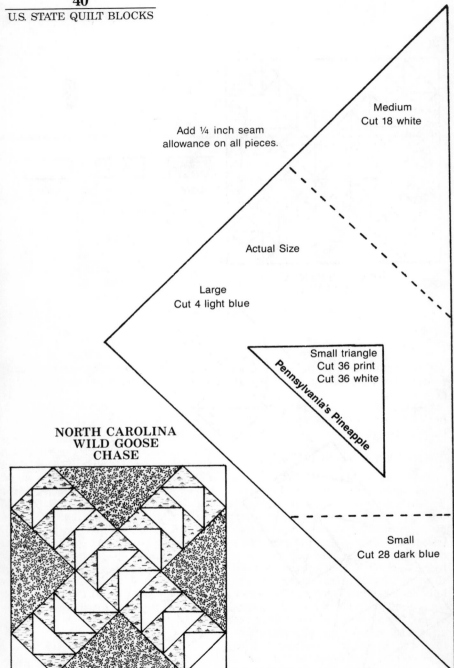

Add ¼ inch seam
allowance on all pieces.

Medium
Cut 18 white

Actual Size

Large
Cut 4 light blue

Small triangle
Cut 36 print
Cut 36 white

Pennsylvania's Pineapple

**NORTH CAROLINA
WILD GOOSE
CHASE**

Small
Cut 28 dark blue

MONTANA
SOUTH DAKOTA

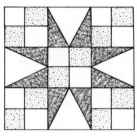

MONTANA
54-40 OR FIGHT

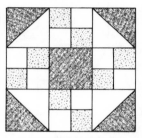

SOUTH DAKOTA
PRAIRIE QUEEN

The Montana and South Dakota quilt patterns are interesting patterns, yet easy enough for a beginner. Triangles and small squares combine to form the basic 4 inch square used in both designs. Completed blocks measure 12 inches.

MONTANA 54-40 OR FIGHT

Montana's 54-40 or Fight resembles a flower when the smaller triangles are worked in green with white and light colored squares. **Add ¼ inch to all pattern pieces for seam allowances.** Cut 8 green triangles on actual size pattern. Place pattern on fold of white fabric for 4 larger triangles. Cut 10 light colored and 10 white 2 inch squares. Sew white and light colored squares to form five 4 inch squares. Stitch a green triangle to each side of the white triangles to form the other 4 squares. Combine the squares to form 3 strips and join as shown. Following diagram, join 3 squares to form a strip; then, sew 3 strips together for

completed block. Alternate with plain blocks or add borders to each block.

SOUTH DAKOTA
PRAIRIE QUEEN

The **Prairie Queen of South Dakota** is a combination of a solid color, print and white. **Adding ¼ inch for all seam allowances,** cut one 4 inch solid colored square, 4 solid colored triangles (½ of 4 inch square), 4 white triangles (½ of 4 inch square), eight 2 inch print squares and eight 2 inch white squares.

Sew print and white squares to form four 4 inch squares; sew solid colored triangles and white triangles to form 4 more squares. As shown in diagram, sew 3 squares together to form a strip; 3 strips to complete the block.

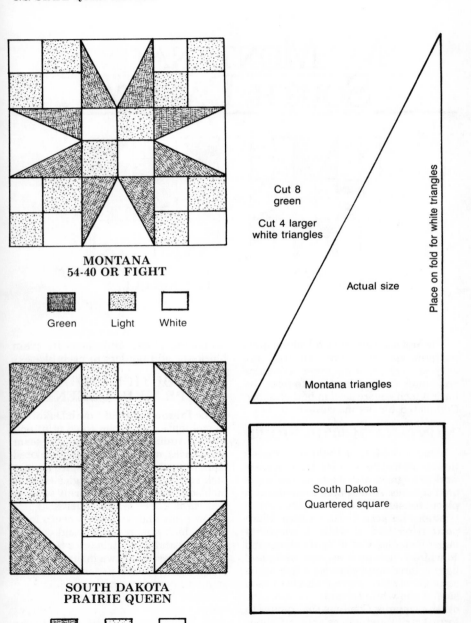

**MONTANA
54-40 OR FIGHT**

Green Light White

**SOUTH DAKOTA
PRAIRIE QUEEN**

Solid color Print White

Cut 8
green

Cut 4 larger
white triangles

Actual size

Place on fold for white triangles

Montana triangles

South Dakota
Quartered square

South Dakota triangle not shown.

MAINE · VERMONT

**MAINE
SPREADING
PINE TREE**

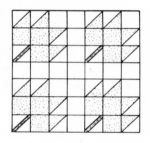

**VERMONT
MAPLE LEAF**

Maine and Vermont (the featured block on our cover) are two New England states noted for their beautiful autumn leaves. Each of their respective state quilts depicts this natural wonder.

MAINE
SPREADING PINE TREE

Maine's Spreading Pine Tree may be worked in light and dark green fabrics with a brown tree trunk against a white background. All pattern pieces are given actual size. **Add ¼ inch seam allowance on all pieces.**

Five identical leaf sections, which form the crown of the tree, should be sewn first. See leaf section diagram for placement and colors. Each section requires 4 dark green leaves, 2 light green leaves and 4 light green half leaves, used at the edge.

After sewing the five sections together, add the tree trunk and white corner pieces. Appliqué roots as shown on pattern piece. This 12 inch block can be set with strips or alternating blocks. If alternating blocks, quilt the plain blocks in the same design as the pieced blocks for a beautiful quilt.

VERMONT MAPLE LEAF

The **Vermont Maple Leaf,** also 12 inches square, can be worked in a summer color scheme of green and white, or use shades of orange and white for a fall look. This easy-to-work block requires only the actual size square and triangle patterns, given actual size.

Sew print triangles to white triangles to form 16 squares (total of 49 squares). The small squares can be arranged in either of two ways. One, work 9 squares to form each leaf. Join 4 leaves with white squares to complete the block. Or, join 7 squares to form a strip, following diagram for correct placement. Sew 7 strips together. Appliqué bias strip for stem. This block can be set as an all-over design or set with strips.

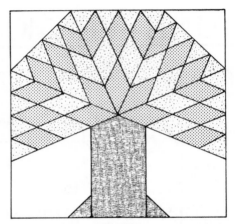

**MAINE
SPREADING
PINE TREE**

 Brown   Dk. Green   Lt. Green   White

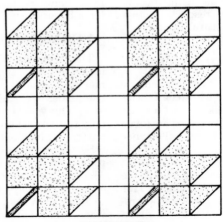

**VERMONT
MAPLE LEAF**

 Dark   Print   White

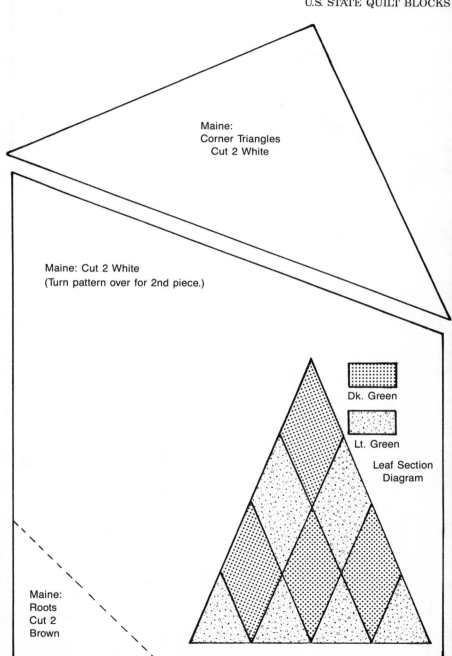

Maine:
Corner Triangles
Cut 2 White

Maine: Cut 2 White
(Turn pattern over for 2nd piece.)

Dk. Green

Lt. Green

Leaf Section
Diagram

Maine:
Roots
Cut 2
Brown

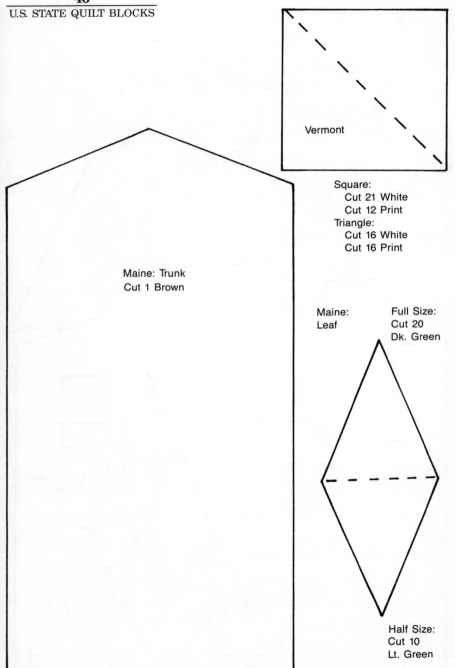

Vermont

Square:
    Cut 21 White
    Cut 12 Print
Triangle:
    Cut 16 White
    Cut 16 Print

Maine: Trunk
Cut 1 Brown

Maine:
Leaf

Full Size:
Cut 20
Dk. Green

Half Size:
Cut 10
Lt. Green

COLORADO
NEW HAMPSHIRE

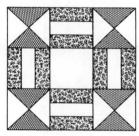

**COLORADO
ARROWHEAD**

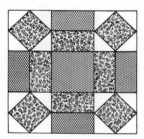

**NEW HAMPSHIRE
GRANITE ROCK**

Colorado's and New Hampshire's 12 inch quilt blocks are each comprised of 9 smaller blocks. Rectangles, triangles and squares surround the center 4 inch square. No curves or intricate pieces to cut and sew!

COLORADO ARROWHEAD

Colorado's Arrowhead is pretty in red, white and blue with the arrows and center square worked in white. In addition to the actual size patterns given, you will need 1 white 4 inch square. **Add ¼ inch seam allowance on all pattern pieces.**

Sew 2 red rectangles to each white rectangle forming four 4 inch squares. Sew a blue triangle to each white triangle forming first a larger triangle; then, sew 2 larger triangles together to form each 4 inch corner square. Following diagram, arrange 4 inch squares to form 3 strips, which sewn together complete block.

NEW HAMPSHIRE
GRANITE ROCK

New Hampshire's Granite Rock can be worked with white, a print and a dark fabric. In addition to the triangles and squares given on the actual size pattern, you will need 1 dark 4 inch square, 4 dark 2 x 4 inch rectangles and 4 print 2 x 4 inch rectangles. **Add ¼ inch seam allowance on all pattern pieces.**

White triangles sewn to each side of the print squares will form four 4 inch corner squares. A print rectangle and dark rectangle will form the side squares. Arrange three 4 inch squares to form strips as shown in diagram. Three strips complete the block.

Both patterns can be used as an all-over design or set with strips.

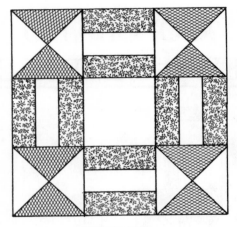

**COLORADO
ARROWHEAD**

Blue   White   Red

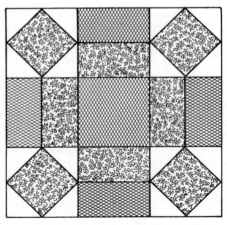

**NEW HAMPSHIRE
GRANITE ROCK**

Dark   White   Print

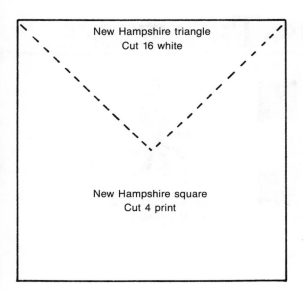

New Hampshire triangle
Cut 16 white

New Hampshire square
Cut 4 print

Colorado
Cut 8 red
Cut 4 white

Actual size

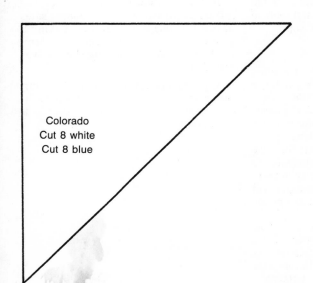

Colorado
Cut 8 white
Cut 8 blue

ILLINOIS·TENNESSEE

ILLINOIS
STAR

TENNESSEE
STAR

Two state quilts based on star patterns are Illinois and Tennessee. Both are a combination of piecing and appliqué. Work the piecing first, finishing with the appliqué. Appliqué using small invisible stitches for a more professional look to your finished quilt or pillow top.

ILLINOIS STAR

The **Illinois Star,** worked in a dark color, white and a print, uses 4 pattern pieces, all given actual size. **Add ¼ inch seam allowance on all pattern pieces.** Beginning with the center pieces, cut 4 white and 4 print. After sewing one white to each print piece, thus forming ¼ of the star, sew 2 pieces together to form halves. Join the halves to complete the star. The larger white triangles will fill in the sides; the dark squares in the corners.

Appliqué the smaller print triangles to the white triangles, covering all but a small portion of the white triangle, as shown in diagram. Set the Illinois Star with strips or as an all-over pattern.

TENNESSEE STAR

For the **Tennessee Star,** you will need a 12 inch white square, 8 pieces A in print and 8 pieces B in a dark color. **Add ¼ inch seam allowance to all pieces.** Being careful to stitch only the longer sides of piece A, form the star, first sewing 2 pieces to form ¼ of the star, then forming halves and then piecing the 2 halves together.

Appliqué each piece B in place along the seams. The entire star is then appliquéd to the 12 inch square. Set the block with strips.

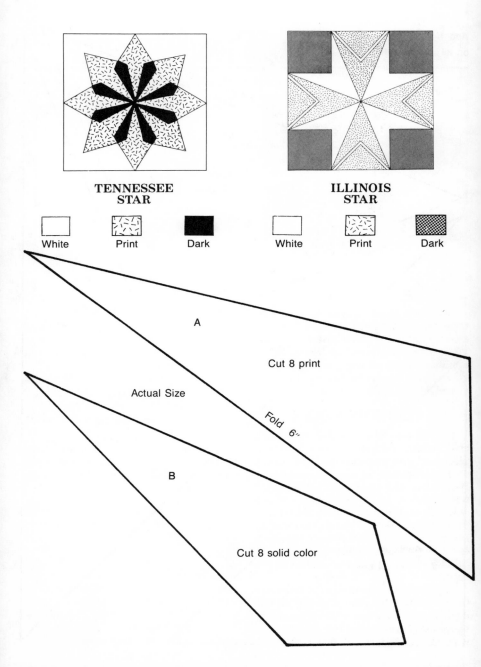

**TENNESSEE
STAR**

**ILLINOIS
STAR**

White   Print   Dark

White   Print   Dark

A

Cut 8 print

Actual Size

Fold 6"

B

Cut 8 solid color

Add 1/4 inch seam allowance
on all pattern pieces.

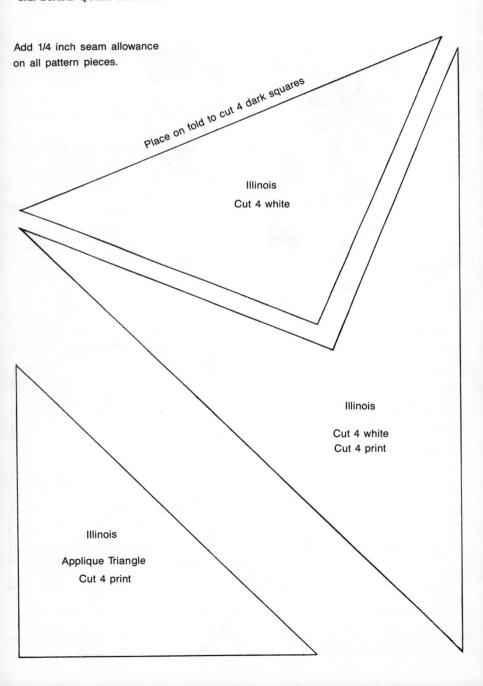

Place on fold to cut 4 dark squares

Illinois
Cut 4 white

Illinois

Cut 4 white
Cut 4 print

Illinois

Applique Triangle
Cut 4 print

WISCONSIN
RHODE ISLAND

WISCONSIN

RHODE ISLAND
PROVIDENCE STAR

The Wisconsin Star and Rhode Island's Providence Star are both 12 inch blocks beginning with a center square, which is then surrounded by triangles to form a larger center square. Both 12 inch blocks start with a center square, which is then surrounded by triangles to form a larger center square. A print, dark color and white fabric are used for both state stars.

WISCONSIN

Wisconsin uses a 2¼ inch center square and 3 different triangles, A, B and C. Cut as directed on each actual size piece. **Remember to add ¼ inch seam allowance on each side.**

Join "A" triangles to center square by sewing base of triangle along each side of square. "B" triangles will be joined together in 4 triangle segments before they are sewn to the center. See triangle diagram for color placement. When the 4 triangle segments are complete, sew the print base to each side of the square.

Complete the "B" triangles by sewing the seam between the white and dark triangle.

Corner pieces will also be sewn individually and then added to finish the block. Sew print "C" to white "C" triangle, forming a square. On each side of the print side of the square, sew white "C," thus completing corner piece. Sew in place.

RHODE ISLAND
PROVIDENCE STAR

Start **Rhode Island's Providence Star** with a 2 inch print square. Add a small white triangle on each side to form square. Join larger print squares to each side of the square; then fill in with the large "house-shaped" white pieces.

To form corner pieces, sew a large dark triangle to each white triangle, forming 8 squares. Add 2 of these squares to each small print square. Add remaining dark triangle to complete corner piece. Sew each corner in place.

WISCONSIN

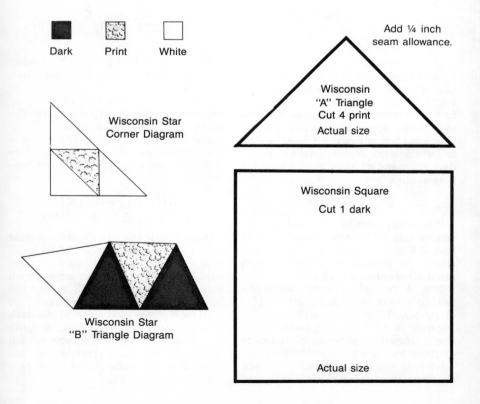

Dark   Print   White

Wisconsin Star
Corner Diagram

Wisconsin Star
"B" Triangle Diagram

Add ¼ inch
seam allowance.

Wisconsin
"A" Triangle
Cut 4 print
Actual size

Wisconsin Square
Cut 1 dark

Actual size

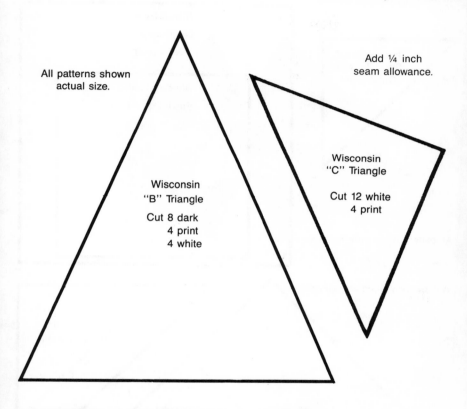

All patterns shown
actual size.

Add ¼ inch
seam allowance.

Wisconsin
"B" Triangle

Cut 8 dark
4 print
4 white

Wisconsin
"C" Triangle

Cut 12 white
4 print

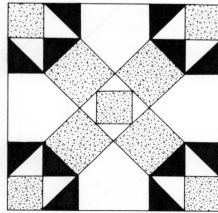

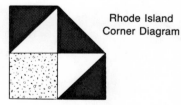

Rhode Island
Corner Diagram

**RHODE ISLAND
PROVIDENCE STAR**

Dark

Print

White

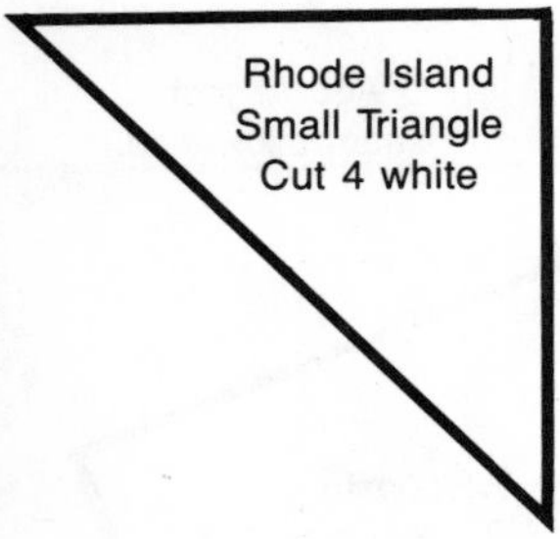

Rhode Island
Small Triangle
Cut 4 white

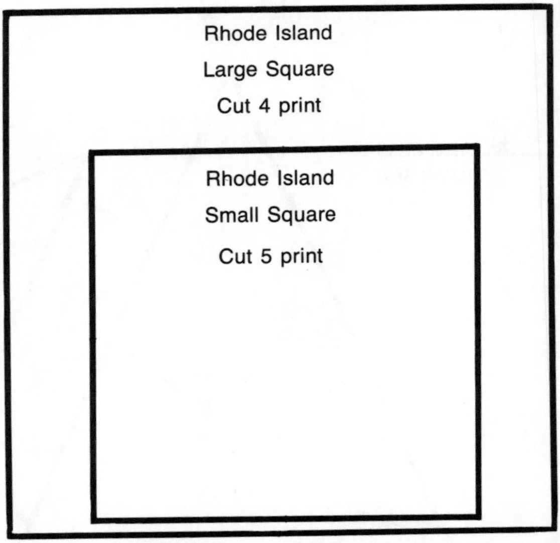

Rhode Island
Large Square
Cut 4 print

Rhode Island
Small Square
Cut 5 print

All pattern pieces are full size.

Add ¼ inch seam allowance.

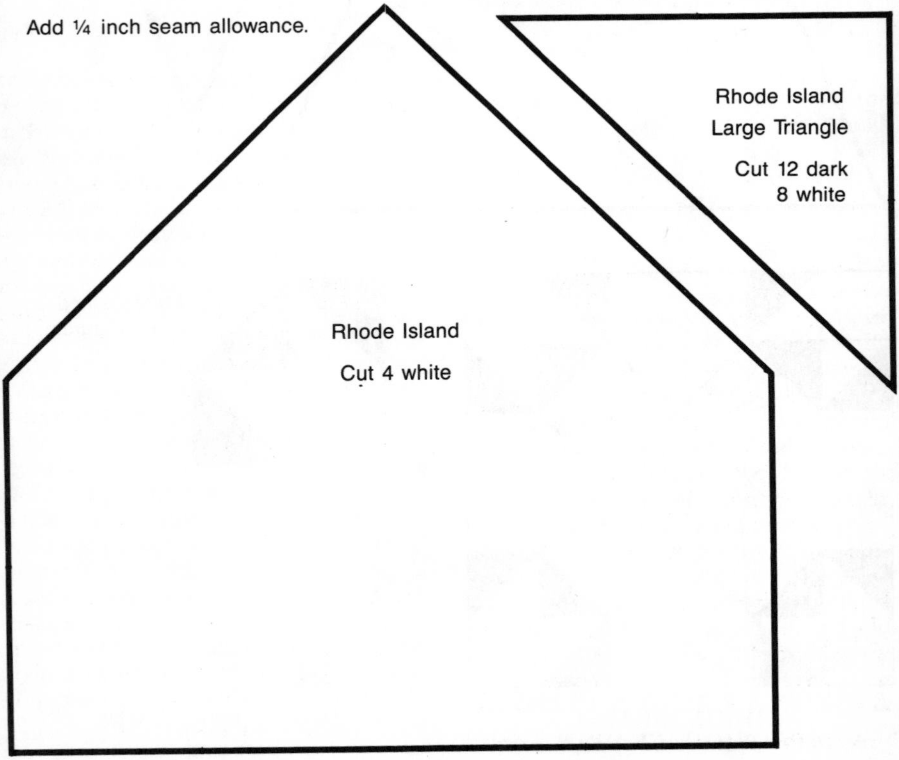

Rhode Island
Large Triangle

Cut 12 dark
8 white

Rhode Island
Cut 4 white

OHIO · ARIZONA

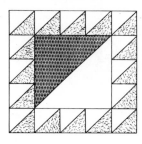

**OHIO
BUCKEYE STAR**

**ARIZONA
CACTUS FLOWER**

Ohio and Arizona both have an inner square surrounded by a bear paw variation. Each 12 inch block uses 3 fabrics.

OHIO BUCKEYE STAR

Ohio's Buckeye Star, using only 2 pattern pieces, is much simpler than Arizona's Cactus Flower. Cut triangle pieces as directed on each pattern piece, **adding ¼ inch on each side for seam allowance.** Sew the two larger triangles together to form the inner square, and the smaller white triangles to the print triangles to form 16 small squares.

Join squares to make two 5 square strips and two 3 square strips. Sew each of the 3 square strips on opposite sides, being sure to place print along the dark side and white along the white side. Complete the block by adding the 5 square strips on top and bottom, still placing the print with the dark and the white along the white side.

ARIZONA CACTUS FLOWER

Arizona's Cactus Flower is worked with either a solid green or a green print for the stem and a pink print or a yellow print for the blossom. The stems form the inner square and the blossoms are formed by the outside triangles. All pattern pieces are given actual size. **Add ¼ inch seam allowance on each piece.** Place one green stem horizontally across the middle of the other stem and sew in place to form the center cross section. In each of the corners, sew a larger white square. Add the diagonally cut stems along each side. Finish the inner square by sewing a large triangle in each corner.

To begin the blossom section (bear paw variation), sew each print triangle to a white triangle to form a square. Join 4 squares following diagram for placement and sew along one side with print towards center. Repeat on other side. Make 2 more 4 square strips, adding a white square on each end. Sew in place along top and bottom to complete block. Sew with strips or alternate with plain blocks. Plain blocks may be quilted in same design as pieced blocks.

**ARIZONA
CACTUS FLOWER**

White   Green or   Pink or
             green print   yellow print

White   Dark   Print

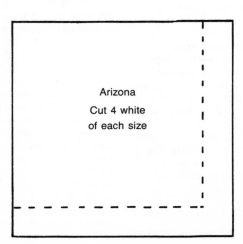

Arizona

Cut 4 white

of each size

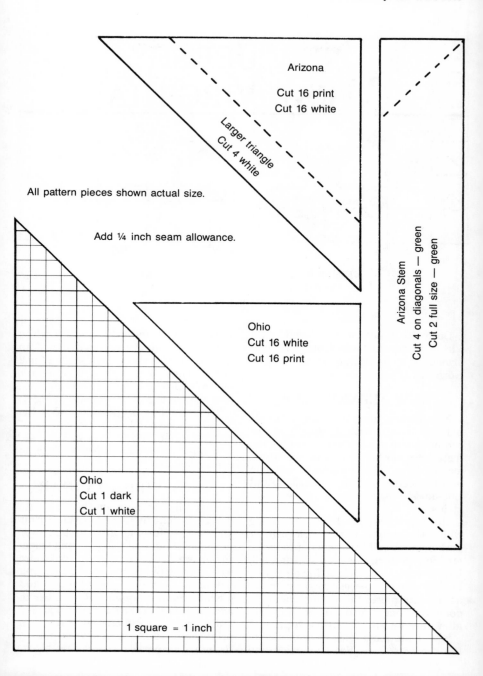

Arizona

Cut 16 print
Cut 16 white

Larger triangle
Cut 4 white

All pattern pieces shown actual size.

Add ¼ inch seam allowance.

Arizona Stem
Cut 4 on diagonals — green
Cut 2 full size — green

Ohio
Cut 16 white
Cut 16 print

Ohio
Cut 1 dark
Cut 1 white

1 square = 1 inch

NEW JERSEY
WEST VIRGINIA

**NEW JERSEY
STAR**

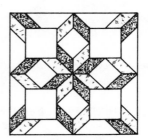

**WEST VIRGINIA
STAR**

Both New Jersey Star and West Virginia Star patterns feature a "four-armed" star and large white squares. Both are 12 inch blocks.

NEW JERSEY STAR

New Jersey Star, a rather intricate pattern, starts with a square in the center and, using squares, triangles and rectangles works its way to the edges, leaving large white squares in each corner. New Jersey's block, also called Aunt Lucinda's block, should be set with strips.

Two fabrics are used, the first being white; the second, either dark print or dark solid. A solid fabric will produce a striking pattern whereas a print will have a softer look. The cutting directions for New Jersey's pieces are given on the actual size pieces, all within the large corner piece. **Add ¼ inch seam allowance on all sides of each piece.**

Sew white rectangles to each side of the center square. Set this aside and

work the 4 "arms" next, using 4 white and 3 dark squares for each arm. Join a white square and a dark square for 2 strips. The center strip will be a dark square with white squares on both sides. Sew 3 strips together as shown in Fig. 1.

Then add the triangles to complete the "arm" as shown in Fig. 2. After 4 "arms" are completed, sew in place around center square. Complete block with large corner squares.

WEST VIRGINIA STAR

West Virginia Star, another intricate design, is done in 3 fabrics (white, print and dark) to form an attractive all-over print. The diamond (piece A) and trapezoid (piece B) pieces are given actual size with cutting directions. In addition, you will need 4 white 3½ inch squares and 4 white 1¾ inch squares. **Remember to add ¼ inch seam allowance on all pieces.**

Join each dark diamond (A) with a print diamond (A), as shown in Fig. 1, to form the basic piece of this block.

NEW JERSEY STAR

When pointed towards you, the dark diamond should always be on the left. Join 2 basic pieces to form ½ of the center star. Repeat for other half; join 2 halves. Set star aside and work 4 "arms" next.

Sew a small white square to a basic piece fitting 2 sides of square as shown in Fig. 2. Repeat with remaining 3 "arms." Sew arms into alternating corners of the star as shown in Fig. 3, sewing large squares as shown by dotted lines. Set aside while working outside edges.

Add white trapezoids (B) to each side of basic piece (Fig. 4). Sew in place along outside edges to complete the West Virginia Star.

Dark

White

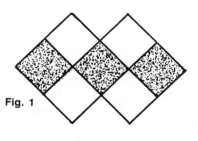

Fig. 1

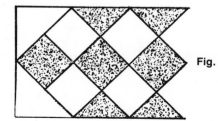

Fig. 2

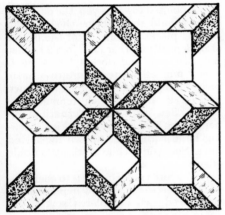

WEST VIRGINIA STAR

 Dark   Print White

Fig. 3

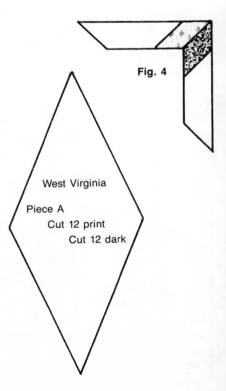

Fig. 4

Fig. 1

Fig. 2

West Virginia

Piece A
  Cut 12 print
    Cut 12 dark

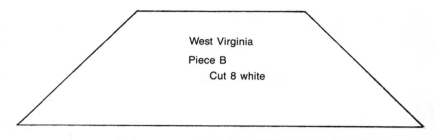

West Virginia

Piece B

Cut 8 white

All pieces given actual size.   Add ¼ inch seam allowance.

New Jersey Pattern Pieces

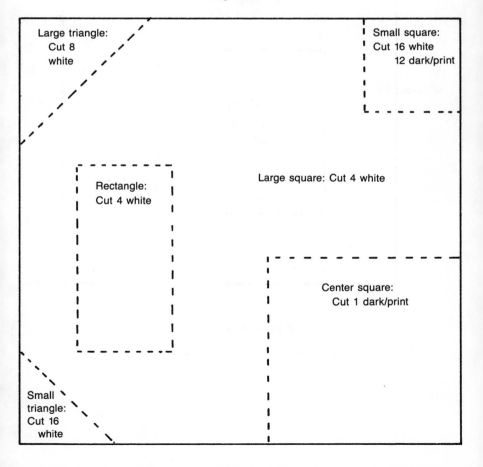

Large triangle:
Cut 8
white

Small square:
Cut 16 white
12 dark/print

Rectangle:
Cut 4 white

Large square: Cut 4 white

Center square:
Cut 1 dark/print

Small
triangle:
Cut 16
white

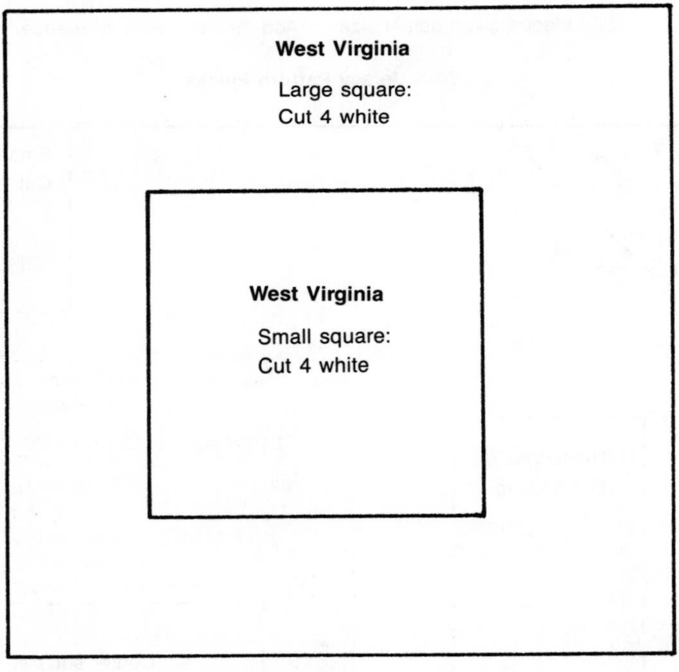

West Virginia

Large square:
Cut 4 white

West Virginia

Small square:
Cut 4 white

Both pieces are actual size.

Add ¼ inch seam allowance.

MISSISSIPPI · MICHIGAN

**MISSISSIPPI
JACKSON STAR**

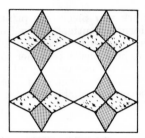

**MICHIGAN
PONTIAC STAR**

Both Mississippi and Michigan's quilt patterns feature four stars on each block.

MISSISSIPPI JACKSON STAR

Mississippi's Jackson Star would be a beautiful way to use remnants. Four small stars provide splashes of color on the otherwise all white pieces. In the original pattern of 1935, Aunt Ellen suggested shades of one color or plain colors and green to resemble flowers. Each block could be different with its own color scheme. Or perhaps, you'd prefer 4 different colored stars on each block, all blocks alike. The choice of fabrics is yours.

All pattern pieces are given actual size with cutting directions on each piece. You will also need 4 white rectangles, each equivalent to 2 of the smaller squares. **Be sure to add ¼ inch seam allowance on all pieces.**

The stars are worked first. Choose 8 diamonds for each star. Sew first into groups of 2; then combine 2 groups to make a group of 4. Combining 2 groups of 4 will complete the star. This method is much simpler than adding 1 diamond at a time. Complete 4 stars.

Sew smaller white square in place between 2 stars. Repeat with other 2 stars. You will still have 6 small squares. Arrange 2 star sections around larger center square. Then add 2 small squares to complete the star section. Rectangles, triangles and remaining small corner squares should be added in that order. Set the 12 inch blocks with alternating plain blocks, perhaps quilted in the same star design as the pieced blocks.

MICHIGAN PONTIAC STAR

Michigan's Pontiac Star is also a 12 inch block with four stars assembled around an octagon instead of a square. To make the octagon, place the long side of the octagonal piece on the fold. To make the four corners, use only ½ of the octagonal pattern. Cutting and fabric directions are given on each actual size pattern piece.

Sew each dark star piece to a print star piece to form 8 identical pieces. Be sure to sew the short seams on the star. Then sew 2 of these pieces together to form the star. After completing all 4 stars, join to center octagon. Add side and corner pieces and Michigan's Pon-

tiac Star is finished. This block makes an attractive all-over design but can also be set with strips.

Because the octagon center is so large, it is recommended that you quilt not only around the edge but also in the center. A decorative circle or star design could be used, or use a more personal design to make this quilt uniquely your own. Michigan citizens especially might want to use quilt designs relative to their state.

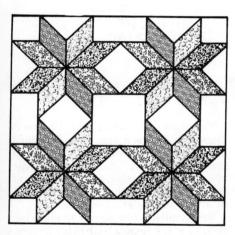

**MISSISSIPPI
JACKSON STAR**

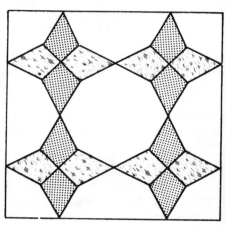

**MICHIGAN
PONTIAC STAR**

Light   Dark   White   Print

White   Dark   Medium

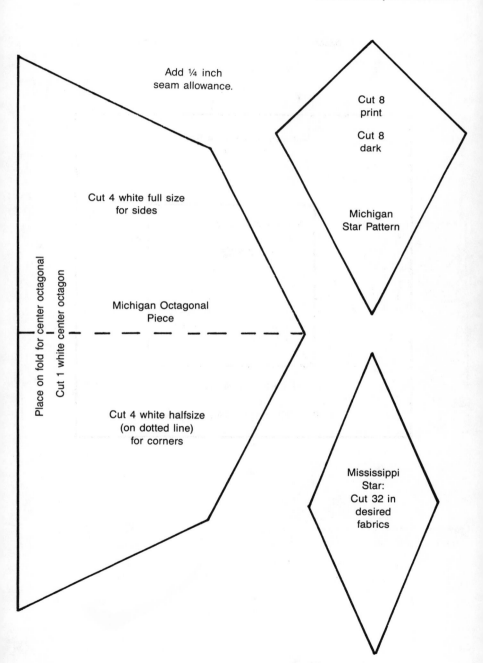

Add ¼ inch seam allowance.

Cut 8 print

Cut 8 dark

Michigan Star Pattern

Cut 4 white full size for sides

Place on fold for center octagonal

Cut 1 white center octagon

Michigan Octagonal Piece

Cut 4 white halfsize (on dotted line) for corners

Mississippi Star: Cut 32 in desired fabrics

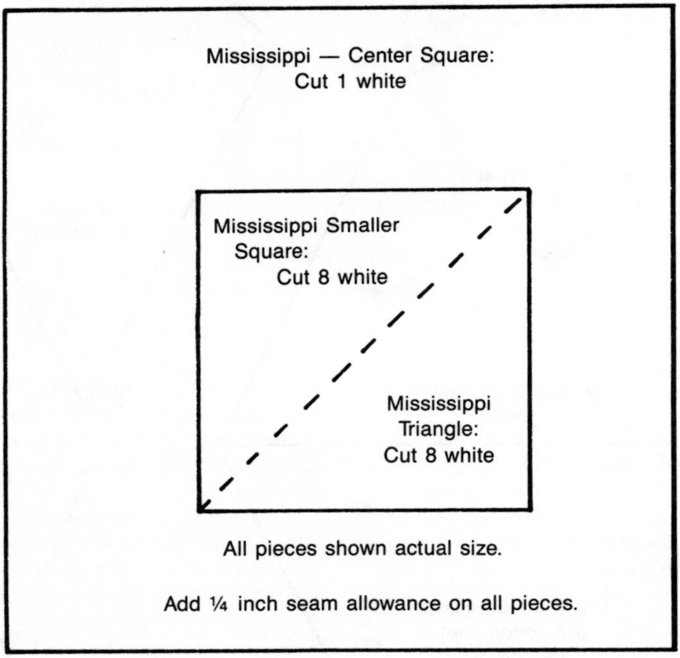

Mississippi — Center Square:
Cut 1 white

Mississippi Smaller
Square:
Cut 8 white

Mississippi
Triangle:
Cut 8 white

All pieces shown actual size.

Add ¼ inch seam allowance on all pieces.

NEBRASKA

NEBRASKA

NEBRASKA

Nebraska's block, worked in red, white and blue as Aunt Ellen suggested in 1935, is so colorful and patriotic — perfect for the 4th of July. Of course, it can also be worked in other colors, perhaps even in pastels. This complex pattern with lots of small pieces includes sections of Bear's Paw and Nine Patch. Taken each section at a time, it's not really as difficult as it may at first seem.

Except for the center 4 inch white square, all pattern pieces are given full size with cutting directions included. **Remember to add ¼ inch seam allowance on all pieces.**

Divide the pattern into center square, 4 corner sections and 4 side sections. Set the center square aside and begin the side sections first. Each side section is further divided into 3 parts. Piece A is complete as cut. The second part is made of 1 piece B with a piece of C on each end to form a rectangle the same size as piece A. The third part of the side section is composed of 2 white piece D's

with blue piece D between them. It, too, will be the same finished size as piece A. Arrange 3 pieces as shown in details of side section. Repeat for 3 other side sections.

Next, begin the corner sections. Using 5 blue piece E and 4 white piece E, arrange in 3 strips; sew 3 strips together to form 9-patch. Each corner needs two 9-patch and 2 small stripe sections. Join 2 white F with blue F to form stripe section. Arrange 9-patch with stripe sections as shown in corner detail.

Bear's Paw is worked next using piece G. Join a red triangle to each white triangle to form 5 squares for each corner. Sew 2 square strip to blue and white corner section. Add 3 square piece along other side to complete corner. Be sure to sew Bear's Paw section with red triangles in position shown in detail. Repeat for other corners.

Now assemble 3 strips; two will be corner, side, corner sections; middle one will be side, center, side sections. Set with strips or make a beautiful Nebraska pillow.

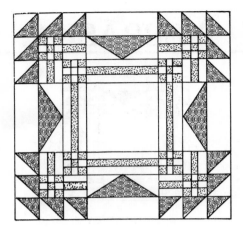

NEBRASKA

 Red White Blue

Corner Section

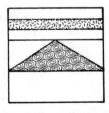

Side Section

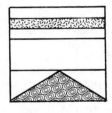

Optional Side
Section

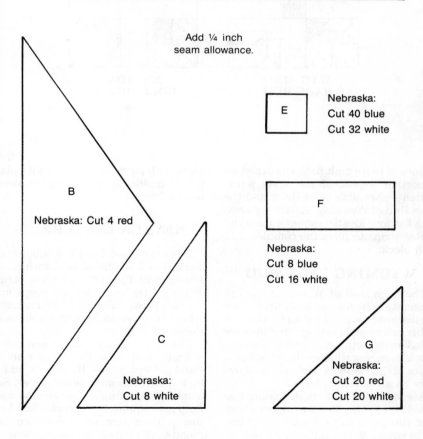

A

Nebraska: Cut 4 white

Add ¼ inch seam allowance.

E

Nebraska:
Cut 40 blue
Cut 32 white

B

Nebraska: Cut 4 red

F

Nebraska:
Cut 8 blue
Cut 16 white

C

Nebraska:
Cut 8 white

G

Nebraska:
Cut 20 red
Cut 20 white

D

Nebraska:
Cut 8 white
Cut 4 blue

WYOMING · NEVADA

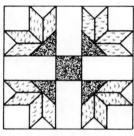

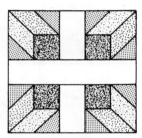

**WYOMING
SAGE BUD**

**NEVADA
GOLD BRICK**

Both of these quilt patterns depict an important aspect of the state represented — Nevada's Gold Brick and the Sage Bud of Wyoming. Relatively easy, each has four identical squares joined by center strips to form the completed 12 inch block.

WYOMING SAGE BUD

The **Sage Bud of Wyoming** can use remnants — prints, solids or both — for the diamond pattern that forms the bud. Other colors and cutting directions are found on the actual sized pattern pieces. In addition, you will need four 5 x 2 inch white strips. **Add ¼ inch seam allowance on all pattern pieces.**

Assemble the buds first, joining diamonds into pairs. Two pairs form a bud. Add the green calyx (base of bud) and fill in square with white square and triangles. Join 2 bud squares with a white strip. Make the long strip with green center square and 2 remaining white strips. Join 2 halves to long strip. Set

block with strips or alternate with plain blocks, quilted in same design as pieced blocks.

NEVADA GOLD BRICK

Nevada's Gold Brick's 4 squares are worked in 3 shades of gold with cream triangles and joined with white strips. If you prefer, triangles and strips may be the same fabric (either cream or white) in order to keep the gold brick dominant.

Cut two 5 x 2 inch strips and one 12 x 2 inch strip in addition to the actual sized pattern pieces. **Be sure to add ¼ inch seam allowance on all pieces.** Sew a medium and light diamond to each deep gold square. See diagram for placement. Then sew seam between diamonds. Add triangles to each corner to complete brick square. Join 2 bricks with small strip, adding last strip in center of two halves to complete the full sized block.

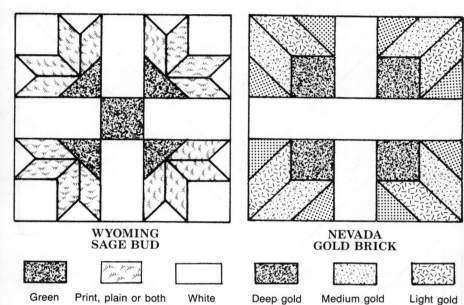

**WYOMING
SAGE BUD**

**NEVADA
GOLD BRICK**

Green   Print, plain or both   White   Deep gold   Medium gold   Light gold

Cream   White

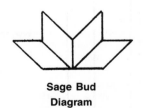

**Sage Bud
Diagram**

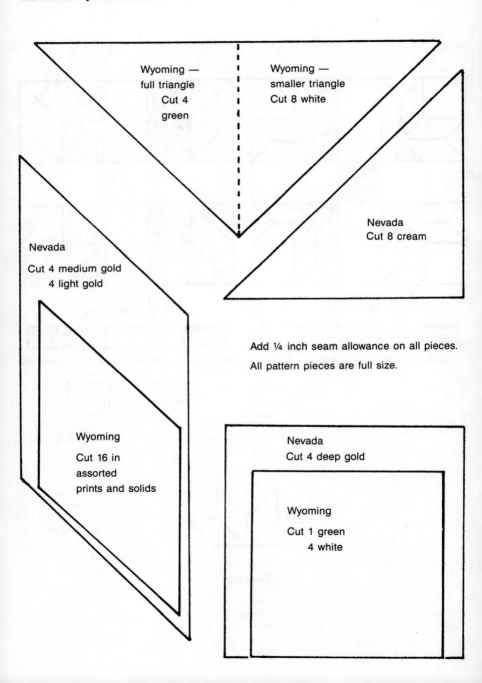

Wyoming —
full triangle
Cut 4
green

Wyoming —
smaller triangle
Cut 8 white

Nevada
Cut 8 cream

Nevada
Cut 4 medium gold
4 light gold

Add ¼ inch seam allowance on all pieces.
All pattern pieces are full size.

Wyoming
Cut 16 in
assorted
prints and solids

Nevada
Cut 4 deep gold

Wyoming
Cut 1 green
4 white

MINNESOTA · NEW YORK

**MINNESOTA
BLAZING STAR**

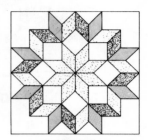

**NEW YORK
KNICKERBOCKER
STAR**

The quilts of Minnesota and New York both feature bold star patterns worked from the same diamond shaped pattern piece. The white exterior pieces and the white squares of New York's block set off three shades of your favorite color.

Each quilt block can be used as an all-over design, with strips or alternating with solid blocks. You will also need 4 white 3½ inch squares.

MINNESOTA BLAZING STAR

The **Blazing Star of Minnesota** was originally designed using 3 shades of yellow, the lightest in the center surrounded by the darkest. Use the medium shade for the points of the star. Pattern pieces are given actual size. **Be sure to add ¼ inch seam allowance** and follow cutting instructions on each piece.

Four diamonds — 1 light, 1 medium and 2 dark — make up 8 larger diamonds. See diagram for placement. Two diamonds make a quarter of the star. Sew 2 quarters together to form one half. Join halves. Diamonds and squares along edges complete the 12 inch block.

NEW YORK KNICKERBOCKER STAR

New York's **Knickerbocker Star** is a more intricate star. The actual sized pattern pieces are complete with cutting instructions. **Add ¼ inch seam allowance on all pieces.**

Begin with center star of 8 light colored diamonds. Join 2 diamonds; then 2 pieces to form one half of the star. A straight seam between the two halves completes the center star. Add 8 white squares as shown.

Next, sew a dark, medium and light diamond, as shown. There will be 8 of these pieces, which will fit around the squares. Sew in place, sewing seams between the dark and light diamonds last. Complete 12 inch block with small triangles and corner pieces.

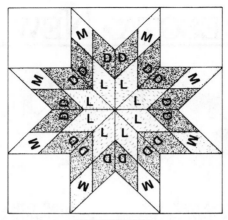

**MINNESOTA
BLAZING STAR**

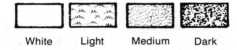

White   Light   Medium   Dark

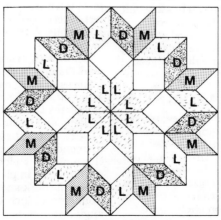

**NEW YORK
KNICKERBOCKER
STAR**

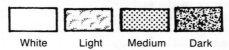

White   Light   Medium   Dark

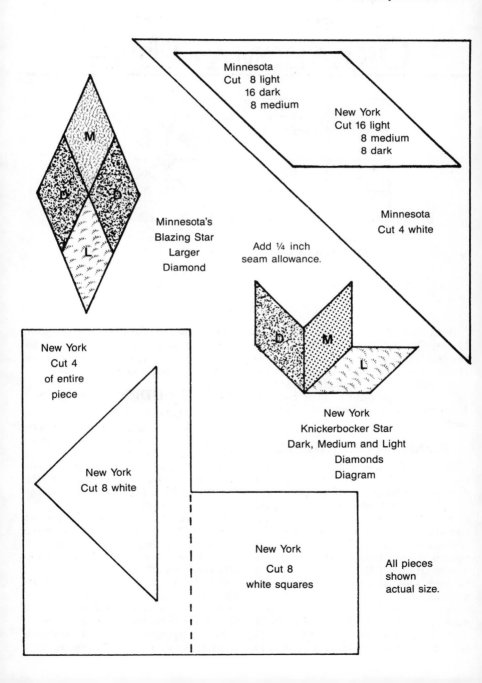

Minnesota
Cut 8 light
16 dark
8 medium

New York
Cut 16 light
8 medium
8 dark

Minnesota's
Blazing Star
Larger
Diamond

Minnesota
Cut 4 white

Add ¼ inch
seam allowance.

New York
Knickerbocker Star
Dark, Medium and Light
Diamonds
Diagram

New York
Cut 4
of entire
piece

New York
Cut 8 white

New York
Cut 8
white squares

All pieces
shown
actual size.

OKLAHOMA · UTAH

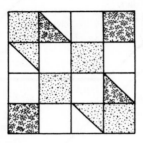

**ROAD TO
OKLAHOMA**

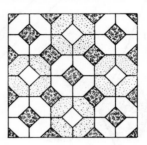

**UTAH
OGDEN CORNERS**

Both the Road to Oklahoma and Utah's Ogden Corners quilts can be worked in either 2 or 3 colors. We have chosen the 3 colored versions for our state quilts. Each is a simple design that will make a splendid all-over pattern. Each block when completed will be 12 inches square.

ROAD TO OKLAHOMA

Road to Oklahoma: If you decide to use only 2 colors, both the print and dark in our diagram will be the same.

For our 3 color version, you will need 6 white 3 inch squares, 2 dark 3 inch squares and 4 print 3 inch squares. The triangle used is equal to ½ of a 3 inch square. You will need 4 white, 2 dark and 2 print triangles. **Be sure to add ¼ inch to each side of each piece for seam allowances.**

Sew each white triangle to either a dark or a print triangle, thus forming 4 more 3 inch squares. There are now 16 three inch squares. Arrange 4 squares to form a row according to the diagram. Repeat until the 4 rows are complete. Then sew the 4 rows together to complete the Road to Oklahoma block.

UTAH OGDEN CORNERS

Utah's Ogden Corners has even more possibilities for variety. Piece A can be cut all from one color, from 2 colors or from remnants, using dozens of prints and colors. The over-all look can also be changed by changing the colors of the squares. With a little imagination, the varieties are endless.

Our block has 3 colors: white, print and dark. The pieces are all given actual size, with cutting directions on each piece. **Remember to add ¼ inch seam allowance on all sides.**

Sew 2 piece A's together. Into the 90° angle formed, place a dark square (Fig. 1). Sew 2 more piece A's together. Add this piece to complete the octagon.

Make 5 octagons with white and dark squares, 4 with print and white squares.

There will be 9 octagons arranged in 3 rows of 3 octagons. Check the diagram for placement and sew 3 octagons together. Add 2 connecting black squares.

Add next 3 octagon row. Repeat with connecting squares and final row. Fill in edges with larger triangles, corners with smaller triangles.

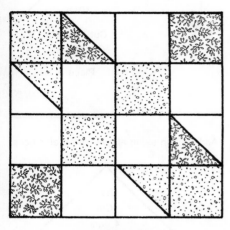

ROAD TO OKLAHOMA

UTAH OGDEN CORNERS

White   Dark   Print

White   Print   Dark

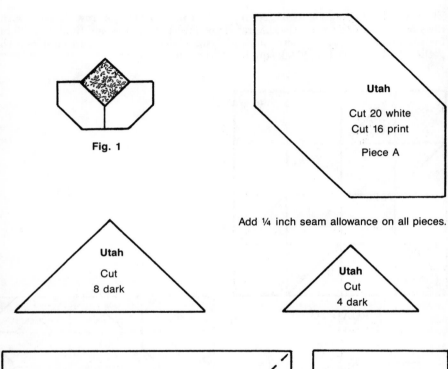

Fig. 1

Utah

Cut 20 white

Cut 16 print

Piece A

Add ¼ inch seam allowance on all pieces.

Utah

Cut
8 dark

Utah

Cut
4 dark

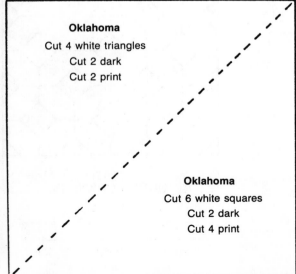

Oklahoma

Cut 4 white triangles

Cut 2 dark

Cut 2 print

Utah

Cut
9 dark

Cut 4 white

Oklahoma

Cut 6 white squares

Cut 2 dark

Cut 4 print

FLORIDA

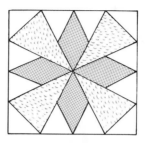

**FLORIDA
KEY WEST BEAUTY**

In the cold of winter, many people dream of a warmer climate. This quilt pattern will bring warmth along with thoughts of Florida's palm trees and sunny beaches.

FLORIDA
KEY WEST BEAUTY

Florida's Key West Beauty is a fairly simple pattern using 3 colors and 4 pattern pieces. The 3 triangles and diamond patterns are all given full size with the cutting directions on each piece. Triangles B and C will be cut on the dotted lines. **Remember to add ¼ inch seam allowance on all sides.**

The pieces can be joined in many ways. The following sequence is recommended because all the seams will be straight, with no angles or corners to sew.

Sew 2 triangle B's to each diamond to form a large triangle (Fig. 1). Sew 1 triangle C to each triangle A to form a large diamond (Fig. 2). Joining 1 large triangle to a large diamond will form ¼ of the complete block (Fig. 3). Join 2 quarter blocks to join a half; then, 2 halves to finish the block.

The 12 inch block can be used as an all-over pattern or finished with strips.

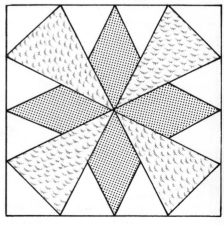

**FLORIDA
KEY WEST BEAUTY**

White   Dark   Print

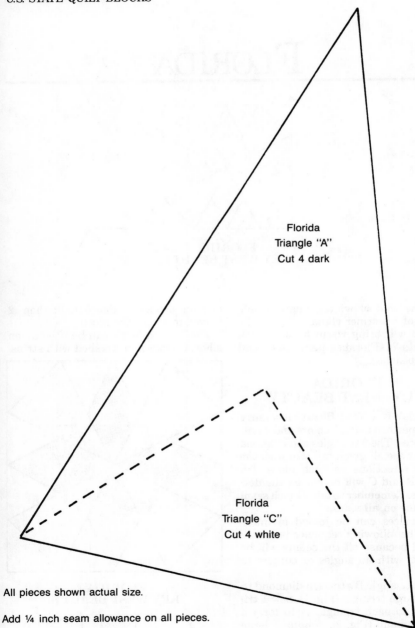

Florida
Triangle "A"
Cut 4 dark

Florida
Triangle "C"
Cut 4 white

All pieces shown actual size.

Add ¼ inch seam allowance on all pieces.

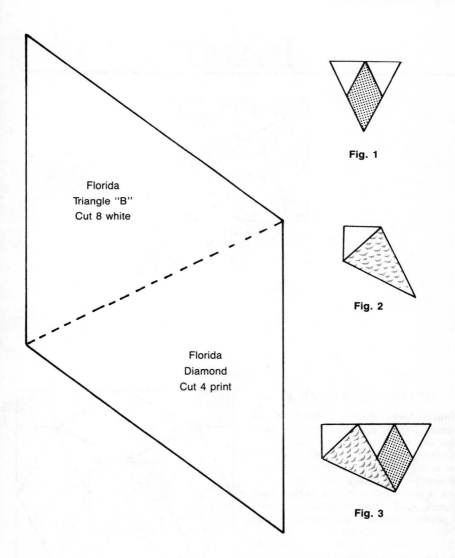

Florida
Triangle "B"
Cut 8 white

Florida
Diamond
Cut 4 print

Fig. 1

Fig. 2

Fig. 3

All pieces shown actual size.

Add ¼ inch seam allowance on all pieces.

IDAHO

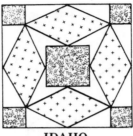

**IDAHO
GEM BLOCK**

IDAHO GEM BLOCK

Idaho's Gem Block or **Arrowhead** is a 12 inch block worked in 3 colors: white, print and dark.

Cutting directions are given on the actual sized patterns. In addition to the pattern pieces given, you will need 1 dark 4 inch square and 4 dark 2 inch squares. **Add ¼ inch seam allowance on all pattern pieces.** Place piece B on fold to cut large diamonds.

The large dark square is the center of the block. Sew pattern A on each corner of the square. Then, sew the large diamonds (B) in place. Set this aside until the corners are pieced.

To work the corners, sew 2 white triangles (C) to each small dark square (Fig. 1). When all 4 corners are complete, sew along outside edge of the diamonds.

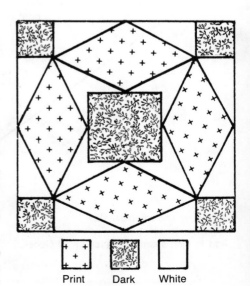

Print   Dark   White

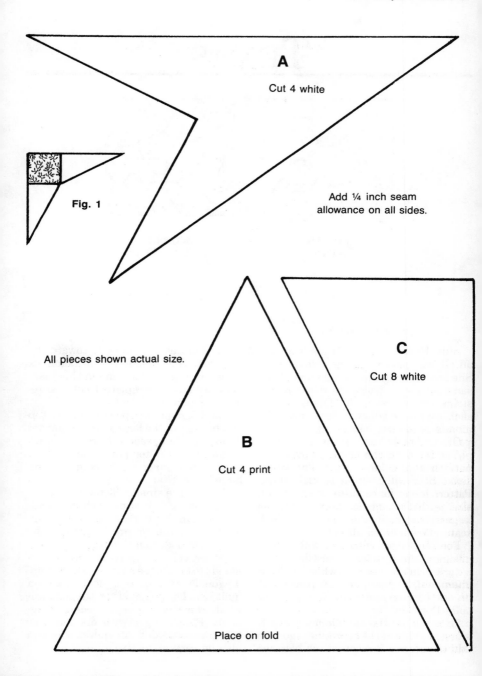

A

Cut 4 white

Fig. 1

Add ¼ inch seam
allowance on all sides.

All pieces shown actual size.

B

Cut 4 print

Place on fold

C

Cut 8 white

TEXAS

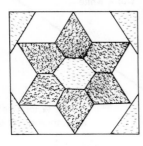

**TEXAS
STAR**

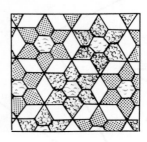

**SMALL
TEXAS STAR**

TEXAS STAR

Aunt Ellen's original **Texas Star** was an all-over pattern using a small star. She recommended working stars of the same color and placing them in diagonal strips across the quilt. The center of each star was yellow, with white diamonds separating the stars.

Our updated version gives the pattern pieces for both the small all-over star pattern and, a larger star. The larger Texas Star will make a 12 inch block. Pattern pieces for each star are given full size, with the smaller pattern on the larger pattern. **Be sure to add ¼ inch seam allowance on all sides.**

For the larger star, you will need 1 medium print or solid A piece (hexagon), 6 dark print B pieces, 4 white C pieces (diamond), 2 white partial C pieces (cut on dotted line) and 4 medium print or solid D pieces.

To assemble the star, join 1 piece B along the side of the center hexagon. To add the second B piece, stitch between

the 2 B pieces from outside toward the hexagon, then along the hexagon as shown in Fig. 1. Continue in this manner until star is complete. Each star requires 6 points.

Sew 4 diamonds in place along the top and bottom of the large star and partial diamonds along each side. See diagram of finished star for placement. Add a triangle in each corner to complete the large Texas Star.

To work the smaller Texas Star, complete 2 stars; join stars with diamond. Continue in this manner to form a diagonal strip. After several diagonal strips are assembled, join the diagonal strips together, continuing to use white diamonds to divide the stars. Work as many diagonals as required, depending on quilt size. The diagonals on the ends will be shorter than the longer center diagonals. Finish edges with diamonds or triangles as needed. An uneven edge can also be very attractive.

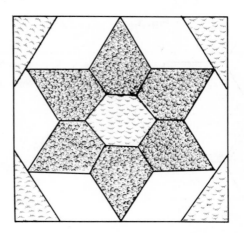

**TEXAS
STAR**

White   Dark   Medium

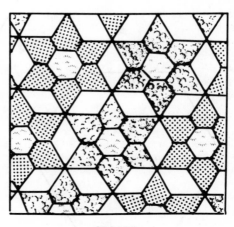

**SMALL
TEXAS STAR**

Yellow   Medium   White   Dark

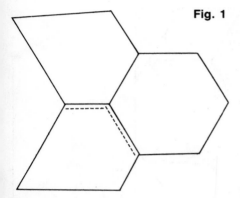

Fig. 1

Add ¼ inch seam allowance on all pieces.

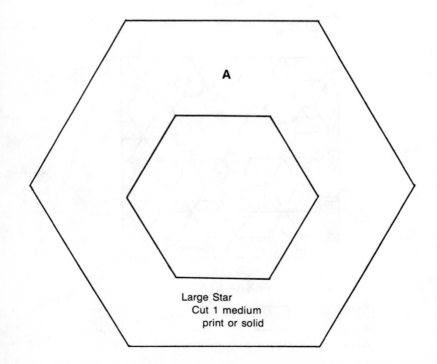

A

Large Star
Cut 1 medium
print or solid

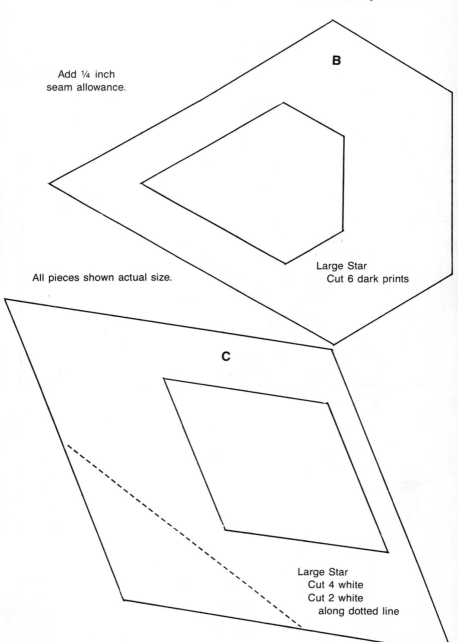

Add ¼ inch
seam allowance.

B

All pieces shown actual size.

Large Star
Cut 6 dark prints

C

Large Star
Cut 4 white
Cut 2 white
along dotted line

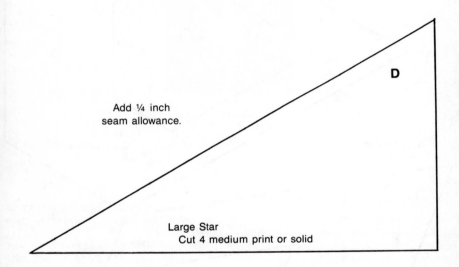

D

Add ¼ inch
seam allowance.

Large Star
Cut 4 medium print or solid

ALASKA

**ALASKA
SNOWFLAKE**

ALASKA SNOWFLAKE

From the ice and snow of beautiful Alaska comes the state quilt block **Alaskan Snowflake**. This pattern can be worked with only 2 colors, perhaps a frosty blue solid or pattern for the background and white for the snowflake. Several shades or patterns in white would make an interesting snowflake.

Each pattern piece is given actual size, with cutting directions given on each piece. You will need 8 of each piece for each block. **Remember to add ¼ inch seam allowance on each side of each piece.** The background square will need to be at least 12½ inches square to make a finished 12 inch square.

Join 2 larger diamonds to form 1 quarter of the center (Fig. 1); then join 2 of the quarter sections to form 1 half. Join the 2 halves to complete the center of the snowflake.

To find the center of the background piece, fold the piece in half and then in quarters. Finger crease. The creases will cross in the center. Place the center of the snowflake on the center of the background.

When appliquéing a diamond, the narrow points at each end can be difficult. To make a sharp point, press the tip of the point (at the seam allowance) toward the center. Then press first one seam allowance over the tip, then the other (Fig. 2). You may want to baste the seam allowances in place. If you do, be sure you will be able to pull the basting thread through after you have completed the appliqué.

Appliqué the center of the snowflake in place. Making sure all your seam allowances are folded under, appliqué the smaller diamonds in place. The line from the center of the snowflake needs to be straight through the narrow points of both larger and smaller snowflakes. The tips of the 2 diamonds should touch but not overlap (Fig. 3). Turn the edges under on the squares and appliqué in place as shown in Fig. 3.

**ALASKA
SNOWFLAKE**

White   Dark   Medium

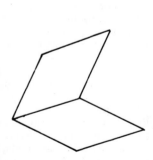

Fig. 1

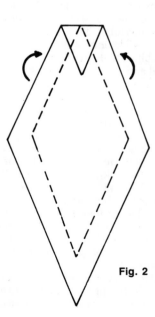

Fig. 2

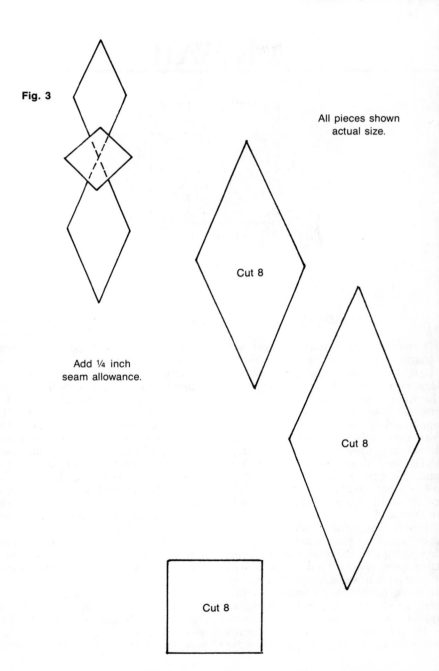

Fig. 3

All pieces shown
actual size.

Cut 8

Cut 8

Add ¼ inch
seam allowance.

Cut 8

Cut 8

HAWAII

HAWAII

HAWAII

Hawaii's pattern uses tropical surroundings as inspiration for its design. Hawaiian quilting is distinctive; often a large overall motif (kapa lau), frequently denoting pineapples, seaweed, coral, tropical flowers or palm trees, is cut and appliquéd to a background. Color combinations, limited to 2 or 3 colors, range from harmonious to bold. Brilliant tropical colors — bright orange, lime, fuchsia and magenta — can be combined to make a striking quilt; often 1 bright color is dramatic against a white background.

Our version of Hawaiian quilting is a combination of palm trees and flowers. In keeping with the other state patterns, the pattern given is for a 12 inch square. If you wish to work a traditional large Hawaiian quilt, however, enlarge the pattern to desired size. Some Hawaiian quilting terms are given in parentheses.

You will need a 13 inch square for the appliqué and another 13 inch square for

the background. Fold background square 3 ways — first horizontally, then vertically and last diagonally. Finger crease. Fold lines should be visible when fabric is unfolded.

Remember cutting snowflakes from paper as a child? Cutting the motif is done in the same manner. Trace the full size pattern onto tracing paper. **The seam allowance is included in the pattern.** Lightly draw the seam allowance line ¼ inch inside the cutting line. The appliquéd square is folded in same manner as background piece. The folded fabric will have 8 thicknesses, with the center (piko) of the pattern at the point. Pin pattern in place starting at center. Be sure to keep fabric smooth as you pin through all the thicknesses of fabric. Sharp scissors will make cutting easier and more accurate.

Baste or press the seam allowance to the wrong side, being careful not to remove the fold lines. Clipping the corners and curves will be necessary to make the motif lie flat. Match the center (piko) of the motif to the center of the background, lining up the 8 fold lines at the same time. Pin in place starting at the center. Baste in place and appliqué. Remove basting thread.

Parallel quilting (luma lau) is often used in Hawaiian quilts. At even intervals of ½ to ¼ inch, work quilting lines following the contours of the pattern. Pattern quilting can be used on either or both the appliqué and the back-

ground. Crossing diagonals can also be used for the quilting design of the background. Perhaps you'd like to quilt palm fronds and the rough bark of the palm tree as shown in Fig. 1.

Borders called leis can be added using the same fabric as the kapa lau. The initials of the quilter or the owner of the quilt are worked in the piko or on a corner.

HAWAII

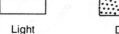

Light   Dark

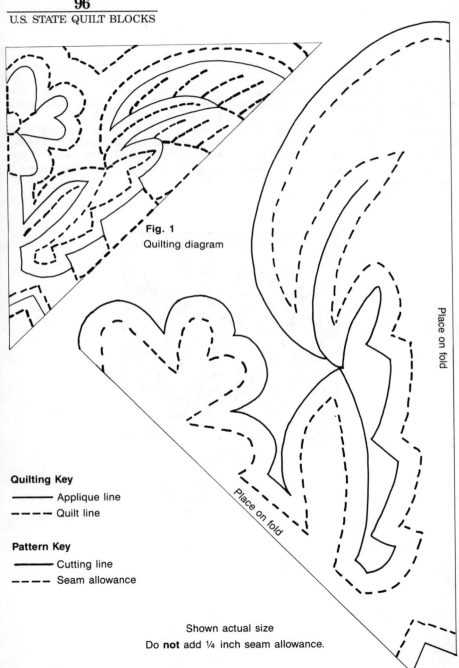

Fig. 1
Quilting diagram

Place on fold

Place on fold

Quilting Key

———— Applique line

- - - - Quilt line

Pattern Key

———— Cutting line

- - - - Seam allowance

Shown actual size
Do **not** add ¼ inch seam allowance.

INDEX